Bruised by Life?

Bruised by Life?

Turn Life's Wounds Into Gifts

Kathleen R. O'Connell, Ph.D.

DEACONESS PRESS
Minneapolis, Minnesota

Published by Deaconess Press, 2450 Riverside Avenue South, Minneapolis, MN 55454

Library of Congress Cataloging-in-Publication Data

O'Connell, Kathleen R. Ph.D.
Bruised by life? : turn life's wounds into gifts / Kathleen R. O'Connell, Ph.D.
p. cm.
Includes bibliographical references.
ISBN 0-925190-32-2 (alk. paper) : $10.95
1. Recovering addicts—Mental health. 2. Compulsive behavior—Patients—Rehabilitation. 3. Self-help techniques. 4. Healing. 5. Self-actualization (Psychology) I. Title.
RC533.033 1994
158'.1—dc20 94-38647
CIP

First printing: November, 1994

Printed in the United States of America
97 96 95 94 7 6 5 4 3 2 1

Cover design: The Nancekivell Group
Interior design: Designsmith
Author photo: Michael's of Whidby Island

Publisher's Note: Deaconess Press publishes books and other materials related to the subjects of physical health, mental health, and chemical dependency. Its publications, including *Bruised by Life?* do not necessarily reflect the philosophy of Fairview Hospital and Healthcare Services or their treatment programs.

The paper used in this publication meets the minimum requirements of American National Standard for Information Sciences—Permanence of Paper for Printed Library Materials, ANSI Z329.48-1984. ∞™

This book is dedicated to

my daughter, Joël, a branch to the future, who patiently

teaches me about love, acceptance,

trust and commitment one day at a time,

and to my namesake

and great grandmother

Catherine O'Rourke O'Connell

a taproot to the past.

Other Books by Kathleen O'Connell:

End of the Line: Quitting Cocaine

"Experiencing the self means that you are always conscious of your own identity. That you know that you can never be anything other than yourself, that you can never lose yourself and never be alienated from yourself. This is because you know that the self is indestructible, that it is always one and the same, and cannot be dissolved in exchange for anything else. The self enables you to remain the same through all conditions of your life."

— *Dr. Carl Gustav Jung*

Table of Contents

Acknowledgments

I would like to extend a heartfelt thanks to a number of people. Special thanks to all my clients through the years, some of whom have contributed portions of their stories to this book.

In addition I'd like to thank Ed Wedman, Jack Caravela, and Julie Odland at Deaconess Press for believing in this project, consistently choosing high quality projects to publish, and standing by them.

Introduction

It was George Bernard Shaw, in discussing the process of writing, who likened a poem to a one-night stand, a short story to an affair, and a novel to a marriage. If this is the case, then this book is also a kind of marriage. It took five years to write and a lifetime to midwife one idea after another, some of which would blossom and others not. Making a commitment to the healing process is a kind of marriage as well, presenting similar kinds of challenges and rewards.

As a society we have come a long way in a very short time. We are now more aware that we have deep wounds which need healing. In 1984, when I wrote my first book, *End of the Line: Quitting Cocaine*, North America and Europe were both in the middle of an epidemic of addiction. Today there are still human tragedies which are the product of drug use, but at the same time there is so much more hope. Now, millions of people understand what it takes to recover from alcohol and drug addiction, and are able to apply those lessons to other traumas in their lives. As a result, we can begin to turn our energies toward the emotional and spiritual healing process itself. The effect on individuals, couples and families can be profound. As a matter of fact, understanding our natural healing process gives us renewed hope for our children and our children's children. It also gives us new hope for society, because we can then see solutions for people all around us who are hurting.

Because this understanding of emotional and spiritual healing is new, it has not yet been researched thoroughly. Consequently, those who experience this healing process have a big task ahead of them. They must make a kind of braid out of their knowledge about the recovery process, the knowledge that they have about themselves, and their experience of being in a family and a world that is not always in sync with them. These last two are huge areas of life in and of themselves, and the task of braiding them together so elegantly that we can barely see the seam where the braids connect is a huge one. But it is also an exciting and hopeful task.

Because I believe the process of recovery mimics the process of normal emotional growth and development, I also believe that these two processes run along parallel lines and are compatible. Just as we need nurturing in order to mature, people who are wounded emotionally and spiritually need support so they can grow emotionally and spiritually. They need hope. They need to know that it is possible to heal, that others have done so before them. How much clearer their path becomes when they are offered an extended hand from someone who knows their pain; a chain of encouragement and information is passed on. This book is one such hand, and I hope someday you will pass it on to someone else in need, and so on down the line. Because helping another person reminds you how it was. And how it can be.

I use the terms "healing" and "recovery" interchangeably throughout this book—"recovery," in my usage, does not only mean recovery from addiction. There is a process underlying healing that is natural, predictable, developmental and universal, regardless of the type of emotional and spiritual wound.

In the first half of this book I describe that healing process in stages. These are not intended to be rigid, but rather are descriptions of aspects of the process, a framework of vocabulary and agreed-upon definitions to use as a springboard to describe internal processes that are otherwise difficult to articulate.

Healing is a choice to take a path. An invitation. There are milestones along that path that let one know there is progress all along the way. One can anticipate them and acknowledge your progress using these milestones, which are measurable, although not everyone will experience the same milestones in the same order.

Part II of this book addresses aspects of healing that are rarely talked about but about which people often wonder. During the past twenty years I have helped several thousand people in their healing processes, some directly and others through doctors and therapists I have taught. A number of questions and concerns have come up again and again, and I address many of them in the chapters concerning families, creativity, dreams, sexuality, and relapse prevention.

To close the book I address the relevance of the healing model I describe to society, and how the multitudes of people who have experienced it can be a powerful influence for the better in changing a wounded world that is, in and of itself, undergoing a healing crisis.

Individuals who make the choice to heal affect many others beyond themselves. This is something for which we can all be grateful. Personally, I am grateful for the gift of recovery, because it has lead to an ability to share my ideas through words and touch many other people, just as others have given to me through the years. Please feel free to take what you can use from what I have written—what seems to apply to you—and leave the rest.

Gratefully,
Kathleen R. O'Connell
Big Sur, California
January 1993

Milestones in Healing

On Saturday, October 5, 1991, I attended what I considered to be nothing short of a miraculous event. Four thousand sober people were gathered peacefully at a musical concert in the Sedona, Arizona mountains, one of the most majestic spots in the world. David Crosby, Graham Nash, and Jackson Browne headlined the concert. Because it was a fundraiser for a very special school, and because so many of the performers were either in recovery themselves or supportive of recovery, no alcohol or drugs were allowed at the event.

The joy of the people participating in the event was inspirational. There were people of all ages, happy to be there enjoying music and each other.

One of the many amazing things about the concert was that at the end of the day when four thousand people had to be dispersed, not an impolite word was uttered by anyone—this despite the fact that everyone had to line up and wait their turn to be bussed out of the concert area after sitting outside in the hot Arizona sun for the seven hours that spanned the hottest part of the day.

That experience stands in stark contrast to one I had survived some twenty years before. If the Arizona concert was a dream, the Altamont, California concert in 1969 was a nightmare. I was there, providing medical care for the many wounded after a bloody battle occurred during the Rolling Stones' performance. The conflict had been sparked by a mixture of alcohol, methedrine and psychedelics taken by quite a few people, including some bikers who had tried to rush the stage.

If these two large gatherings of people were microcosms of new worlds, I'd naturally choose the world of the Sedona concert. I still look back on that day as a peak life experience—a little taste of what peace in our time could feel like. Call me an idealist, a child of the sixties, but where are we without ideals? The Sedona concert was a powerful example of the positive effect that harmony of purpose creates, and of how profoundly human beings can affect one another.

People in one kind of healing process or another now number in the millions, and I believe that these people are contributing to a kind of global transformation. The change in consciousness that I saw at that concert could be one that spreads throughout the world, just as drug addiction, alcoholism and hopelessness spread throughout communities. Every time an individual chooses recovery, there is cause to feel hope for the world. This hope is a most profound gift for all of us.

Because people often forget that healing is a dynamic and not a static experience, I am placing a list of some of the milestones in healing in this first chapter. If you are going through a rough time as you read this, I hope the list will remind you that it will not last forever—in healing and recovery, change is the order of the day. There is always hope.

Milestones in Healing

- You will break any chains of hopelessness, shame, and secrecy that may have been handed down within your family.
- You will learn to listen.
- You will be able to personally validate yourself and depend less on others to do this for you.
- You will recapture innocence.
- You will see beyond yourself and overcome constant self-absorption.
- You will develop the capacity to feel joy.

- You will be able to experience the present moment.
- You will be free from self-pity.
- You will understand that strength may be found in being vulnerable.
- You will learn about boundaries in relationships.
- You will learn to respect the messages of your own body.
- You will learn to develop self-esteem.
- You will learn from the past—not by getting stuck in the past, but by using your knowledge and awareness about the past as a tool for moving in a healthy way toward a freer future.
- You will be able to make a 100 percent commitment.
- You will learn to pick a partner who can give as well as receive in a relationship.
- You will learn not to settle for a situation or a partner that is not right for you.
- You will see choices in life.
- You will slow down when appropriate.
- You will learn to admit you don't know all the answers.
- You will accept the lessons provided by experience and not fight so hard when a new lesson is presented by life.
- You will learn to get involved in a relationship out of mutual interest rather than out of need or pity.
- You will experience healthy self pride.
- You will create a safe environment for yourself.
- You will feel as if you belong.
- You will have fun.
- You will get your needs met through direct, healthy ways rather than by manipulation.

- You will experience and express feelings at the time an event occurs rather than seventy-two hours to twenty years later.
- You will be honest with yourself and with others.
- You will learn to be alone with yourself comfortably.
- You will be loved for yourself rather than for your achievements.
- You will create stability.
- You will recognize and respect your own inner voice.
- You will have a sense of purpose about your life that is larger than your individual, mundane, day-to-day life concerns.
- You will let go of old resentments.
- You will have to identify fear and how to deal with it in a productive way.
- You will reduce the number of secrets in your life, and their power over you.
- You will gain a sense of personal spirituality that is unique to you.
- You will learn that it is okay to speak up when a situation or event is uncomfortable for you.

You can use this list as an inventory checklist. At the end of it you can mentally leave some space to add more milestones in your own recovery process. I hope you have many, many things to add. People often like to copy this list and put it up where they can see it frequently throughout the day—on a bulletin board or the refrigerator. It can be both a reminder and a barometer of progress.

Human Woundedness and the Nature of the Healing Process

Human suffering and the woundedness that results is a part of life. Simply to function, we must recover to some extent; but the term "recovery" does not do justice to those of us who have chosen to soar beyond the woundedness. The pivotal point created by a deep emotional and spiritual wound can be a source of unlimited strength, the power of which goes beyond recovering from the original damage.

Suffering is universal. It is not the exclusive purview of those of us who have a history of addictions or abuse. We are not "terminally unique"—an expression many of us have heard at one time or another in recovery. But it is true: we are not really so different. In fact, one of the basic ideas behind some of the early thinking about recovery from addiction was that after an individual's basic work on his or her own recovery, that person should return with that knowledge to the mainstream of life.

Healing is Universal

If suffering is universal, so is healing. I contend that it is natural as well; the spirit will heal if placed in a safe, life-affirming environment.

The first step in encouraging this universal process is to make a 100 percent commitment to a positive path of healing. Up to this point in their lives, most people have never made a 100 percent commitment to anything. It is an enormous undertaking. Sometimes a 100 percent commitment means not getting out of bed because the temptation to return to an addiction or an old destructive habit is too tempting. In short, it means that you make healing the number one priority in your life. 99 percent and 100 percent are vastly different when spiritual, emotional, and sometimes even physical health hangs in the balance.

Another characteristic of healing is that it must be freely chosen. Coercion and manipulation, whether imposed by yourself or others, are not effective. You cannot be forced to heal, nor can you force yourself to heal. You must have a motivation that is meaningful to yourself.

Healing is Natural

Over the past twenty years, I have worked with over three thousand people who were undergoing healing of one kind or another. They chose a plethora of different paths only to arrive at the same place. No one path holds the one true answer. No one path is the only key to wisdom or serenity. I have seen people follow everything from a personal path they can't fully articulate to paths involving the twelve steps, meditation, traditional religions of all kinds, and eastern and western philosophies. But they all worked with a 100 percent commitment and their paths all contained the same underlying process—one of allowing healing to occur, providing a structure to think about life, and making positive changes in how life is lived. This natural process allows people to grow up emotionally.

Healing is Predictable

The following process occurs regardless of the path chosen:

1. The person undergoes a crisis. It may not be the first time a crisis occurs, but this time is different because there is a shift in perception; the person realizes that a change must be made and she must make it. I call this momental realization a window of grace.
2. The person sees that there is a choice. Earlier on, the person had a choice, too, but did not perceive there was a choice.

3. The person makes a 100 percent commitment to the chosen path. This is not without some struggle and testing, but the person learns from the struggle and becomes stronger in the commitment over time.
4. A surrender to the path chosen takes place. This means that the person has come to trust the course he has taken.
5. An assessment process is undertaken where the person reviews her life—both positive and negative experiences—to improve as a human being. This often means facing the past in order to right wrongs and tie up loose ends before going on to the future.
6. The person makes a commitment to a lifestyle that is supportive to staying on the path rather than in conflict with it.
7. The person continues to stick to the new way of living and notices some far-reaching positive changes that he wouldn't ever have guessed would happen at the beginning of the process.
8. The person gets back on track quickly when she notices herself drifting.
9. The person can comfortably exist in society at large, having incorporated the new philosophy so completely that it feels natural; it has become a part of him that he does not have to constantly think about.

Healing is Developmental

Many of us are parents. At one time or another we went to the Pediatrician's office and anxiously glanced at the growth and development charts on the wall to see how our children ranked according to the statistics for normal height and weight. The classic books on baby and child care continue to be popular because we need reference points to judge growth.

The same is true of recovery. Fortunately, predictable stages of growth occur during more-or-less predictable time periods. The stages

I have cited are not rigid, but they offer a general guide that is useful and reassuring. I have developed this guide over the past twenty years in treating thousands of people; I noticed and charted common developmental patterns. This guide has proven to be a tremendous source of hope, because people could use the milestones to chart their own progress while having the comfort of knowing the challenges that lie in the future. When you recognize your progress, you can give yourself credit for a job well done.

Woundedness Is Not the Same as Disease

Suppose a person sees that it is a beautiful day and decides to go on a bike ride. A bump in the road is unseen by the rider. An accident occurs. The and incurs an injury serious enough to justify an emergency room visit and a few well-placed stitches. This person, while basically a healthy individual, has received a wound. It will heal in time, because the person is healthy and knows how to care for the wound from both common sense and proper education from the medical personnel at the emergency room. In addition, the underlying health of the person will play a role in the healing process, and nature makes healing a predictable experience for the most part.

Most of us become wounded in one way or another throughout our lives, but being wounded and having a disease are two very different things. This is a subject worth examining in a societal context, where the term "disease" is sometimes used casually and without due consideration of the impact of the word. "Disease" is defined as a particular destructive process in an organism, and a "wound" is defined as hurt to the tissues, the feelings, or to honor. It is important that as a society we develow a language to discuss our woundedness. There is an important and distinct difference between these words.

You might ask what difference a simple word choice can make. Language has a profound effect on how people view themselves. Some of the language drawn from the chemical dependency field is influencing large numbers of people because it has become a part of popular writing and nomenclature. Many conditions are being referred to as diseases when they are not truly disease states. To use the term *disease* as a metaphor is one thing, but to use it literally can result in a powerful and possibly damaging mindset. True, a sufficient body of research documents genetic markers in the case of alcoholism and drug addiction, so they may be referred to as a diseases. *These truly are diseases.* But how about workaholism and sex and love addiction? These conditions are deep wounds as well. However, referring to these and other related conditions as disease states is not only inaccurate, but also disempowering to the millions of people who experience pain and woundedness.

Many people have fought during the past sixty years for alcoholism and drug addiction would be seen as diseases and not moral conditions. It is important to keep this perspective. Otherwise, we will go backwards as a society in the areas of treatment for these diseases. This has already started in some cases. Calling the other conditions diseases confuses people and downplays the need for comprehensive treatment for their conditions.

To believe that someone is basically a healthy individual suffering from a wound inflicted as a result of a number of factors assumes that, as in the case of the cyclist, the wound will heal over time given recognition and proper treatment. The condition is not degenerative.

People with a disease will almost always need medical treatment. Faced with disease, they are no longer the primary experts on their own bodies and must turn themselves over to someone else's expertise. This compromises their own power and deep sense of what is healing for them. (This disempowerment is an old story, especially for women, who still are the majority of those treated on both in and outpatient basis for "psychiatric illnesses." And while legitimate diseases certainly exist, some conditions are based on patterns of habit, learned over time.

When I hear the term *codependence,* I think about woundedness rather than disease. I choose to define the issue as "alienation from self" rather than refer to it as an illness. This book is about people learning to heal their own wounds.

People who are wounded spiritually and emotionally are like the bicyclist. They are wounded, not diseased. They are the experts on their own psyches, their own woundedness, and their own healing.

Stage I in Healing and Recovery

Stabilization Corresponds to Infancy

Stabilization is the achievement of firmness of purpose and firmness of character. The following is an example of that process:

Several years ago, a bright, attractive woman walked into my office. Sarah wanted to rid herself of two things that were, in her estimation, dragging her life down. One was alcohol (white wine in her case) and the other was a long-term pattern of dating emotionally abusive men who generally had drinking problems also. She was in her early forties, had a good professional job, was divorced and the mother of three grown children.

Sarah made a 100 percent commitment to staying sober and treating herself well. One month after her first appointment she came in and told me the following story:

"Three weeks into my sobriety I went out on a blind date with a lawyer. We met at a restaurant where we spent the first hour and a half in the bar with another couple—friends of his. After a few peripheral questions he inquired if I wanted a cocktail or champagne, which was already on the table. I said, 'I'll have a Perrier.'

He responded, 'So, you don't drink?'

'No.'

'Not at all?'

'No.'

This exchange ended with his response, 'Well, that's a strike against you,' as he raised his gin on the rocks and took a long swallow.

"During the next hour and a half I endured his endless talk about himself, with few acknowledgements to me. I quickly came to the conclusion that this man was a raging bore with a personality that consisted of everything that I dislike in a man.

"It was decided the four of us would go to the other couple's house for dinner. That appealed to me; it meant I wouldn't have to eat dinner with this man alone. Then I found out they lived over an hour away.

"About 7:30 p.m., after Mr. Wrong had downed about three—maybe four—drinks, the other couple exited, telling Mr. W. and me to wait about twenty minutes before leaving because they needed to pick up groceries on their way.

"Then Mr. W. got up from across the table, came around to the side where I was sitting, and sat—not next to me, but practically on top of me, his face was no more than six inches from mine. He launched into a twenty-minute dissertation about all the losers who have worked for him, and how he tried to help them be successful. He continued on as if entranced with the sound of his own voice.

"I sat drinking my Perrier wondering how I would endure over an hour in the car with this creep and thinking that if I was drinking wine, the whole fiasco would have looked quite different. Finally, the words 'I can't do this' crept into my head, then, 'Hey, Sarah, you don't have to do this,' and finally, 'I'm definitely not going with this man.'

"Just about then he jumped up, clapped his hands, and said, 'let's go.' I asked him to sit down because I had something to say to him. He sat. I told him that I wasn't going and that I felt we had a personality conflict. He seemed thrown off balance for a moment and then said, 'Well, I don't like you either.' I replied, 'That's okay,' and got up and started walking out of the bar. From behind me he snarled, 'You know, you're good looking, but you're a wimp. Where's your car, I'll walk you to it.' I told him not to do me any favors. I walked alone to my car and drove away feeling less like a wimp than I had in years!"

When Sarah came to the office and related this story, I asked her what she had learned as a result of this experience. She said that her big lesson was that by saying no to this man she felt better about herself. She said that her self-esteem had been boosted by several notches and that she finally understood what it meant to assert herself. In the past, she said, she would have gone out with a man like the one in the restaurant; he was a typical date for her. As a matter of fact, if she had been drinking, she might even have let herself get sexually involved with someone so emotionally abusive. It was an old pattern. Because she wasn't drinking, however, she could see the situation was not right for her and that she had choices and options. She went ahead and made her own choice and came out feeling better about herself and her recovery than before.

At the time of this writing, it is almost eight years after this incident took place. Sarah is still sober and is in a healthy, loving, committed relationship with a man.

I like to tell this story because it says so much about the essential components of the early stages of healing. It points out several elements in making the kind of commitment that Sarah made and keeping it.

•**The Perception of Choice.** Because healing is predictable, people can start the process as soon as there's a choice to do so. But choice is not a simple thing.

Some people go through a number of crisis situations before they realize that choice exists for them. Others observing them may see choices that the wounded person cannot. (A crisis is sometimes dramatic, but often it is not. The Chinese words for crisis translate into two words in English: One is "danger," the other "opportunity.")

Take Sarah's situation. Nothing dramatic happened to force her to decide to give up drinking and abusive men. In fact, to the casual observer, her life might have looked pretty good. She had healthy, positive relationships with her grown children, a good job, and she owned her own condo.

What *she* saw was something very different. She viewed herself as a once attractive woman who was aging badly. She saw herself as lonely and isolated because she lived alone. She was frightened that she would end up alone—old, afraid, and sick, so she would take emotional abuse from a man because the alternative was the pain and fear of being alone. She tolerated men like her ex-husband and father, both of whom abused and neglected her.

Sarah could have gone on like this indefinitely. Instead, something shifted inside of her. Because of that shift she *perceived* that she had a choice. Others could see that she had always had a choice.

This critical window, when a person finally perceives choice, can open and close quickly. It is a *window of grace*. Grace is defined as an unmerited gift from God. It is a time to seize the moment. Most people who make a major change like Sarah did have a moment like this. It is a precious, magical, fleeting phenomenon. It is a time to *take action*. A time to make the commitment to change.

The danger comes when a person passes the moment by without making a commitment. The opportunity to recognize the feeling that accompanies this shift and take action is lost. Moments like this that are passed over may return, but they are fleeting states of grace and as such, they are unpredictable. And because this shift is a natural, internal phenomenon, no one else can second-guess it. You are the expert.

•**Making a 100 percent Commitment.** Sarah made and stuck with a 100 percent commitment to stay abstinent from alcohol and abusive relationships.

Alcohol and abuse went together for Sarah. She knew that in the past she would have tolerated the man's self-obsessed, emotionally abusive style, and that if she let herself date a man like that, her risk of relapse was great. Because she said no to him, she felt an immediate boost in self-esteem, which in turn strengthened her commitment more. But 100 percent commitment is a level few people experience before having a significant perceptual shift.

As mentioned earlier, sometimes 100 percent means choosing to stay in bed rather than be around temptation or particularly stressful situations in early healing. Remember, 99 percent and 100 percent are not the same. Especially in their first year, people need to be highly dedicated to their healing. After all, a tremendous adjustment needs to be made to a new way of living. Healing must be the #1 priority.

This may sound a little rigid or self-obsessed. It is, at first. But the truth is that nothing less works. Eventually, the new lifestyle becomes so much a part of a person that it feels natural. At first, however, the new lifestyle feels anything but natural.

The dangers here include (but are not limited to) simple forgetfulness, which can lead to relapse or the return of old behaviors. The opportunity looms great. But as in Sarah's case, every time a decision is made in keeping with the 100 percent commitment, self-esteem soars.

•**Mentors and Support.** An infant takes time to learn how to walk. This learning is part of a universal, predictable process, yet it still varies from infant to infant. A few suddenly take off on foot. Most work at walking in stages. They sit up; they receive support from adults to stand; they learn to lean on objects, then they receive support from adults to take that first step. Finally, one day, they can be seen taking that first, solitary step. All of this is predictable, natural, and developmental.

People in the early healing stages are the same. It is natural to feel scared and alone—this is new territory. Like infants learning to walk, people in early healing need the support of others.

When Sarah first started her process of healing she felt alone. She thought she had no one in her life to support and guide her. And in fact, there were a number of people in her life who would not support her new lifestyle. But she made a short list of people who would support her and committed to spending time with them while letting go of contact with the others. In the beginning, she saw me as a mentor to coach her in developing her new life.

A mentor is important in early healing. This can be a friend, relative, counselor, or sponsor—anyone who will support you in this new commitment. Sometimes it takes a while to find that person, but it is worth spending the time. The lonely feelings that occur without a mentor can be particularly intense and dangerous to healing in the beginning. The opportunities presented in finding a mentor are great, because people learn how to value themselves with each new step.

•Support Groups. Early healing can be lonely at first. It takes time to develop relationships with people who are positive and who support what you are doing. Building friendships that are both positive and reciprocal takes time. The skills necessary to build such friendships must be learned. In the beginning, stick with people who will say they will support you and follow through with behavior that is supportive. If what people say they will do is different from what they actually do, they are not truly supportive. Trust can only occur when people are consistent in what they say and do. Still, because no one is perfect, it is a good rule of thumb to look for at least an 80 percent consistency between words and behavior. Look and listen for consistency, both in how people treat you and how you treat others. The danger here is the pain of discovering that some people you know may not be true friends. The opportunity is that you will experience what true friendship is, perhaps for the first time.

•Stability and Physical Health. Infants need rest, proper nutrition and a calm and loving environment to flourish. People in early healing need the same things.

One of the primary tasks of the first stage of healing is physical recovery. (This often extends beyond the first stage as well.) The person in the first stage of healing is struggling not only with their emotional equilibrium, but also with becoming physically stable. The vital organs are recovering, and they need proper nutrition and rest to support this process.

People who are healing must eat a healthy, balanced diet. Often, they must learn to do this for the first time in their lives. They need to become like parents to themselves—to care for and 'baby' their bodies. Eating high-quality food and getting regular exercise are both important parts of emotional as well as physical healing, because they are a part of a deep caring and self-love that is developing.

The nervous system goes through a tremendous adjustment in early healing. This statement seems obvious when applied to people in early recovery from chemical dependency. However, other people who are in early healing go through a similar adjustment as well.

For instance, childhood trauma can leave a person in a state of hypervigilance. As a result, the arousal of their nervous system is constant, like a switch that was turned on long ago and left that way. People who have suffered such trauma often overreact physically and startle easily. Because the body is in a constant state of arousal, adrenaline reactions occur quickly and frequently. While this "fight or flight" response was learned in childhood as a survival mechanism, the reactions often continue into adulthood, even when there is no threat from the outside.

At one time I owned a VCR that turned off and on by itself at times. It happened at random, for no apparent reason. Traumatized nervous systems become this way over time.

People *can* learn to retrain and heal their nervous systems. The first step is to put yourself in a safe living environment, to reduce outside stress and stimulation. The second step is to learn how to lower your pulse via a simple biofeedback technique, because relaxation is the opposite physical response to adrenaline arousal.

Take your pulse and then think of a relaxing visual scene or piece of music. After you feel relaxed, take your pulse again. Repeat this procedure until your pulse is significantly lower than when you began. If you practice this technique, you can use it when you feel that your nervous system is overstimulated to gradually retrain your responses.

The third step in retraining the nervous system is to eat a nutritious diet. Sugar and caffeine stimulate the nervous system. The sooner you reduce your intake of these chemicals the faster the nervous system will adjust. Chemicals interfere with this healing, which is a natural process. After you reduce or eliminate them, the body, in its wisdom, will begin to heal on its own.

•**Brain Repair.** The brain is part of the nervous system and therefore participates on a physical level in natural and predictable healing in early recovery. Help it along by treating your body in a loving way. Regular exercise is important; it stabilizes the blood sugar level, which in turn will make you feel optimistic and more emotionally stable. When the body is treated well, the brain heals itself. The pleasure center of the brain becomes more active, and people report that they enjoy living more than ever.

"Anhedonia" means "a lack of pleasure." This phenomenon is due to some adverse effect on to the pleasure center in the brain. It can be overcome; people in early recovery often report that they are slowly beginning to look forward to each new day. Sometimes people begin to see the world in color where before they saw only shades of gray.

The opportunity here is obvious. The dangers involve impatience. Always remember that things will improve with time. Notice the small improvements and keep a journal noting each one. Give yourself credit for measurable changes.

Memory and concentration will improve with time as well. A woman I worked with—an executive who was recovering from cocaine addiction—was worried that she couldn't write memos. She had trouble putting words together. Over time, however, she noticed improvement. Within fourteen months her verbal and writing skills returned.

Drugs vary in their effects on the nervous system. People also vary in their responses to drugs. Some drugs are stored in the fat cells, and because of this it takes longer for the body to completely purge their toxic effects. The nervous system can take years to completely repair itself from the effects of some drugs. (Marijuana and valium are two examples of these.) People who are recovering from drug abuse need to remember this. Chart your progress over time, and you will see measurable improvement. Journals and charts can be important motivational techniques; they provide reminders of improvement and hope.

Milestones in Stabilization (Stage One)

Here is a partial list of measurable milestones for the first stage of healing. Because everyone is different, there is no rigid pace you must follow—use these as guidelines only.

Feel free to add your own milestones to this list. You can rate yourself periodically on a scale of 1 - 10 for each of these, but don't be too hard on yourself. Remember that improvement is experienced in degrees over time.

- You will learn to give yourself credit for your efforts in a measurable way by journaling, charting, or listing milestones in your healing.
- You will acknowledge your commitment one day at a time.
- You will stay in the present and stop overwhelming yourself with thoughts of the future.
- You will think about yourself in a positive and caring way and stop any negative or shameful "self-talk" inside your head.
- You will learn to feel and acknowledge small pleasures in life.
- You will learn to take good basic physical care of your body by eating healthy food, exercising, and engaging in other measurable behaviors that reflect self-love (Examples: using a seat belt regularly when driving, flossing teeth regularly, and so on).
- You will learn what it is to be a true friend and to have a true friend.
- You will create a safer, calmer environment in which to live and work.
- You will experience improvement in concentration, focus and memory.
- You will learn to be honest with yourself about your needs.
- You will learn self-forgiveness when you have fallen short of a goal.
- You will learn to be more open and honest with others about who you are and what your needs are.

- You will learn to respect other people and their rights and opinions.
- You will learn to say no to people and situations that are not positive and healing for you.
- You will learn to respect your body and to take care of it when it is hungry, cold, or tired.
- You will learn to seek emotional support from people who are caring toward you.
- You will begin to identify and cope with emotions like anger, sadness and fear, which are signals that you need support.
- You will begin to identify what kind of support you need in different situations.
- You will recognize signs of stress and seek extra support at these times.

Every time you acknowledge a milestone, healing and self-esteem receive a boost. Set aside a few minutes every day to go over this checklist.

Stage II in Healing and Recovery

Deepening Corresponds to Toddlerhood

Deepening is defined as extending far downward, inward, or backward in self-discovery.

One of the hallmarks of Stage II recovery is that people begin to understand more about themselves. Like toddlers, they want to experience and try new things. They realize that a new way of living encompasses more than the commitment to stop doing something self-destructive. They may feel a void because while they no longer want the old way, their new philosophy of living is unclear. This is all part of the development of a strong identity.

In order to develop new ways, people need to have changed old attitudes. They must be aware of old behaviors that now cause them a lot of pain. (Before people are ready to change a behavior, they often talk about it. This is because attitude change precedes behavioral change, and people need to talk in order to form new attitudes.)

Six years ago, Tony began treatment. He had decided to stop using cocaine and alcohol. In six years he learned a lot about himself. He wrote the following story about himself after two years of recovery. His story illustrates how people who want to change talk about it before they actually do change. It also shows how people often stop one or two destructive behaviors before they are ready to change other behaviors that are also not working anymore.

"Two weeks ago, a lady I used to date during my divorce showed up out of the clear blue sky. I was immediately suspicious, but proceeded to ask how she was. She confessed a myriad of problems in her life; financial, personal, etc. She also admitted that her drinking and drug use had escalated in the last six months.

"Well, the old light bulb went on immediately. I decided that I was going to help this girl turn her life around to AA. I asked her to come in on Saturday night and have dinner with me so that we could discuss this more. She had had no idea that I was in the program, but when she found out, she was very attentive to what I had to say.

"I have to admit that my interest in helping her was not altogether altruistic. We had had a good physical relationship three years ago, and I was curious to see if there was that possibility again, although it was far in the back of my mind.

"The next night she came in for dinner and we talked for hours. I told her the rewards of AA without trying to do any pushing. She listened, but it was obvious that she was still in denial. All through dinner she drank. I could see the changes in her, and I remembered why I had stopped seeing her before. She was not a pretty sight when she was drinking.

"At that point I gave up; another part of my brain had kicked into gear. During my recovery I have felt fresh out of the womb when it comes to sex, relationships, and just living. I rationalized that perhaps having sex would enhance my recovery as well as my self-esteem.

"I invited her over to my abode, and her response was a quick 'yes.' Her rationale was that she was going to be moving soon and she wanted to check out where I lived. Right! I wasn't the least bit affectionate or flirtatious—as a matter of fact, I was kind of turned off by her drunken behavior. We watched TV for about one hour, during which time she undressed and put on one of my T-shirts.

"We had sex, and it was satisfying to me because I thought I performed rather well. The only thing missing was the cigarette dangling out of the corner of my mouth—I don't smoke. But then she said she felt I had only used her for a physical release, and it bothered her. My honest response to her was, yes, I had. But what did she expect? I thought she had been after the same thing. "Anyway, she left the next morning after I made up a story about having a brunch date. I just wanted her out of there. I told her I would go to an AA meeting the following week with her if it would help, but I never heard from her again.

"I felt good about going to bed with her, but guilty (I think) about using her. I'll probably do it over again, but at least I was honest about my feelings. I guess she couldn't handle that. But who used whom?"

Tony talked a lot about his relationships with women during the last three months of his first year of sobriety. He indicated that he was not pleased about the way he related to women and that he wanted to change this about himself.

In the past he really had not let himself feel deeply in his relationships with women. He wanted this to change in sobriety, but he didn't know how to do it. So, like many people who want to change some old familiar behaviors and attitudes, he started by verbalizing the new attitudes first. Tony talked in therapy about not wanting to pick up women and have casual sex with them anymore before he was ready to stop doing it. Several months later he had the experience with the woman from the bar and he learned from it. He had tried to behave the way he used to before he was sober, but it didn't fit him anymore.

The following are some factors in encouraging and experiencing the deepening stage of healing:

Behavioral Change

Adopting a new behavior is like going to a department store to try on gloves. You may have to try on a number of pairs before you find a pair that fits you well. Then, even the pair that fits may take a little while to break in. They must adapt and mold to the shape of your hand over time.

Tony first talked about changing his attitude toward women and relationships. Then Tony went back and tried an old behavior (picking up a woman and having casual sex) that didn't feel right anymore. Next, he began to explore other ways of behaving based on attitudes he was just learning. It was time for him to try out some new behaviors to find ones that worked for him. In Tony's case, he met a woman named Martha and got involved in a close monogamous relationship.

Tony is married today, the father of a lovely baby girl. It took a while for Tony to identify a new lifestyle that did feel right for him, and at first it didn't feel completely right simply because it was something different—something new. Still, he knew it was a good fit, and it began to feel natural over time.

Still, as the relationship with his wife has deepened, Tony has come into therapy a number of times. There are times when he describes that part of him is kicking and screaming, wanting to get out of the relationship, yet this is not how he feels most of the time. Most of the time he wants to stick with the relationship because it is a solid, healthy one. It is such a new experience for him to make a commitment to one woman that he is stumbling his way through it. But he is getting a lot of support from other friends in AA, his therapy, and newer friends in his life who are also involved in committed relationships. He is listening to these new friends and learning from their experiences.

Sexual Response in Early Healing and Recovery

Like many other men in early recovery, Tony's first stage of recovery was marked by some disconcerting experiences for him in the area of sexual response. Tony was surprised to find that he went through a period of time where he had difficulty achieving and maintaining erections during sex. This physical symptom was a part of his changing attitudes about relationships and his new awareness that he was dissatisfied with casual, one-night-stand sexual encounters. His body spoke loud and clear—he was not responding anymore to this transient kind of stimulation. This prompted him to look at his attitudes toward women and toward relationships.

In the first year of recovery, the body is still in repair on many levels. Part of this repair affects sexual response. Men usually experience a return in desire and sexual response during the first year. Problems encountered during the first months of healing are usually temporary, but should be looked into medically if achieving or maintaining erection is a continued problem.

Women, too, sometimes experience a period of time when they are either less interested in sex or less able to experience physical sensations in their pelvic region during sexual activity. This is called "pelvic anesthesia"; it is not unusual during early recovery. It is a transient phenomenon that occurs more frequently with women recovering from cocaine addiction than those healing from other kinds of trauma. This is also a condition that should be looked into medically if it persists.

Often, on the psychological level, there is a need to devote a period of time to develop new attitudes toward relationships, sexuality, and what sexual response means to the individual. Also, an element of shame may occur for people who are healing if they have done or said things in the past that are against their own value systems.

Many people have had experiences that they look back on with some degree of shock, and a feeling that they are onlookers remembering someone else's life and not their own. This is the kind of situation where same-sex support groups can be very helpful. In the private area of sexuality, people are often more likely to open up and talk about private matters with those of their own sex rather than in a mixed group.

Tolerating Intense Feelings

In the second year of healing, some people experience emotional crises. Old feelings from childhood often surface; without the old behaviors to suppress them, these feelings are free to emerge. Nonchemical addictions and destructive behaviors cause alterations in consciousness and emotional numbing just as chemicals do. People healing from any self-destructive behaviors can experience these newfound intense feelings.

Two of the feelings that people avoid most often are fear and sadness. Instead of retreating to self-destructive behaviors, however, it is important to reach out for support from someone who understands what it is like to have strong feelings emerge. Tony is a good example of this, because in his second year of recovery he began to have a lot of memories surface that he had not experienced since his early childhood. Tony's father was alcoholic and very much an absent figure emotionally for Tony. He spent a lot of time grieving for his lost relationship with his father. But by experiencing these strong feelings, Tony learned that he could tolerate feelings and not be overwhelmed by them. He could experience strong feelings and not need to use drugs or alcohol to suppress them or escape from them. Sadness by itself has never killed anyone, and yet the attempt to escape from sadness through drug use or other self-destructive behavior *does* kill people. A task of the second stage of healing is not only to identify feelings, but to learn to tolerate experiencing feelings.

Feelings are not the enemy. As a result of their new learning, the person in the second stage of healing learns that a wide range of feelings may be experienced. This can be a big surprise because when people are still using chemicals or some other destructive behavior as an escape, the feeling range very often becomes narrow. In recovering from trauma, people experience the shades of gray and many subtle permutations of feelings between the extremes. During this time, it is important to remember that a person who can feel deep sadness is also a person who is capable of feeling great joy.

Tony was a good example of a person whose range of feelings had been limited. He said once that he had never realized before that he actually saw the world in several shades of gray, with very little color. Seeing the world in color is a metaphor for rejoining the world in the second stage of healing.

There is a children's story called *The Wind in the Willows*. In the story a rat comes to visit a mole who, like most moles, lives under the ground. The mole decides to join the rat in a journey along a river to visit another animal called Toad. When Mole first leaves the lower world and joins Rat in the upper world, he is astounded by the color, by the shapes and the trees and the grass. He is amazed by the sounds—especially by the sound of the wind in the willows. This kind of wonderment at reconnecting with life and celebrating life is a hallmark of the second stage of recovery. You remember—or realize for the first time—life is full of joy and wonder.

Optimal Physical Health

In the second stage of healing, the body naturally strives toward optimal physical health. For the most part, the primary physical detox for those who are recovering from drug addiction takes place in the first year—but not all of it does. For people who have used drugs that are stored in the fat cells, like marijuana, PCP and valium, it takes another six months to a year for the body to release all of these toxins.

But whether or not substance abuse was involved, it is not unusual for people in the second year of healing to really begin to feel good physically (perhaps even for the first time in their lives) and to celebrate that feeling of wellness. So it is only natural to become more physically active and to become more concerned about the quality of food one eats. All of this indicates a new interest in living—a lifestyle rather than a "death style." And as a result of this new exercise and diet, people feel better. This in turn affects their healing and often helps stabilize their emotions. When a person is taking good care of their body they are more likely to be stable physically and emotionally.

One of the gifts of the second stage is to reach beyond basic physical recovery to high-level physical wellness. When people reach toward physical wellness that is optimal for them, their self-esteem increases because they know that they are attending to their inner voice. In the second stage, people are more in touch with themselves and attentive to the guidance of their inner voice. The second stage of healing is often a good time to get involved in various types of body work and massage therapies, because these types of therapies not only help people to get in touch with their bodies and minds, but to become more fully aware of how the two are connected.

Renewal of Commitment

In the second stage an increased commitment concerning recovery occurs. This may mean different things depending upon each person's path of healing. People who are in self-help groups like AA often experience a renewed commitment to their program and a deeper understanding of the meaning of the program. That is why this stage is called *deepening.* They are now ready to really work the steps of the twelve-step programs and do closer, more in-depth work with their sponsor or mentor. For people not in twelve-step programs, this second stage of recovery can mean a renewed commitment to understanding themselves through a number of tools, such as keeping a journal, attending workshops to learn more about themselves, taking more time off from work to really enjoy life, and perhaps considering an involvement with some other type of therapeutic process.

In the second stage, people come to understand that they have made a 100 percent commitment to their recovery, so that whatever is going on in their lives, they still maintain that commitment. For people in recovery from chemical dependency, that means to stay clean and sober one day at a time. For people in recovery from other kinds of wounds, that can mean implementing a variety of ways of setting your priorities and taking good care of yourself.

This stage corresponds to the toddler because, like a toddler, the person in stage two wants to explore new ideas and feelings. The base of support must be firm in order to try new things, but opportunity lies in this exploration. However, potential danger lies there as well. Toddlers without guidance can end up exploring a light socket with a piece of metal or an open flame with their hand. A person in stage two of healing still needs guidance to avoid the jolts and hurts life can offer.

Coping with Boredom

Another task in second stage healing is learning to cope with boredom. If boredom is attributable to a lack of awareness, however, the whole perspective on the notion of boredom is changed. For instance, Tony came in to me in the second stage of his recovery and explained that he was bored with his relationship. When I asked what he meant by being bored, he said that they did the same things all of the time and there didn't seem to be a big variation in routine. The relationship was becoming predictable and he was concerned because in the past he routinely would leave relationships at this stage. He didn't want to do that anymore.

When someone who has only been involved with a person for a few months says, "I'm bored with this new relationship," they are facing a kind of restlessness that is internal. Their boredom really has nothing to do with their partner. People who have this kind of internal restlessness often project it on their partner and decide to separate, yet that restlessness has nothing to do with the partner.

When Tony came in with this complaint, he was encouraged to take a look at what was going on inside himself. In Tony's case, this restlessness had to do with a fear and a sense of despair deep inside himself that he could never really be intimate with anybody. This sense of despair went back to his childhood and his relationship with his parents. He could see that his parents were never really close to one another and never really intimate with him, either. As a child he really did not have an example to model in terms of intimacy. Also, the ability to be intimate requires a sense of internal wholeness that he didn't have yet.

I asked Tony, "Was there someone whom you had some contact with as a child and whom you wanted to be like?" He said there was—a friend of the family who had had a good marriage and happened to be his Godfather. Tony had spent a lot of time with his Godfather's family as a child. As a matter of fact, Tony had spent so much time with this family that he often complained about having to go home; he knew instinctively that this other family had something he wanted. He talked about this family and the kind of love and acceptance that was present in their relationships with each other. Tony was able to capture that intimacy and security that he had had early on, and he reached deep inside himself to use his knowledge of that feeling in his current relationship.

Tony wanted to experience the feeling of intimacy that he recognized in his early childhood. As soon as he was able to recognize his despair about ever being intimate and to talk about some of these early experiences with his Godfather's family, the feeling of boredom lifted. He no longer felt internally restless, and he was able to go back to his relationship with a renewed sense of wonder and hope.

Most people have been presented with healthy role models at some time in their lives. These role models do not have to be parents in order to be effective role models for intimacy.

This tendency to feel internally restless and to want to cure this restlessness by changing something in the outer world is very common. It is important to identify whether the restlessness is internal, and if so, acknowledge that it has nothing to do with anyone or anything else. For when restlessness is internal, solutions must be internal as well. This kind of boredom is not a genuine feeling; it is a cover-up for some other, deeper feeling like despair, longing, sadness, anger, or fear. When people acknowledge the feeling underneath the boredom, they are halfway to changing the situation. This kind of awareness is a very powerful tool.

Feeling Stuck

Another example of this kind of internal restlessness came up a few years ago with another person who came to me for counseling. Tom was in the second stage of recovery. He had a very good marriage, yet had begun to feel the sense of internal restlessness that people often feel in the second stage of recovery. Instead of facing the restlessness for what it was, he had decided that perhaps it was time to think about getting a divorce. At this point he came in for a session to discuss what was going on in his life. This was a very wise move; he was coming in to examine his situation rather than taking quick action and getting a divorce as a quick cure for something that turned out to be an internal problem. The truth was that he was feeling stuck.

People often get the feeling of being stuck when some emotional "detox" is occurring. For example, Tom's feeling of being stuck in his marriage came at a time when he was experiencing a lot of memories flooding from his early childhood. Tom had been sexually abused by his mother and the pain and shame were just beginning to become conscious for him at this point. The discomfort he was feeling was in his relationship with himself—it had to do with some internal issues that he needed to work on.

People in the second stage of healing often have deep internal issues like this that come up as a result of them beginning to remember events that happened in their childhood—events that are coupled with strong feelings. Earlier in his life, Tom did not have the recollection that he had been abused. He only knew that he didn't remember most of his early childhood. In the first stage of his recovery, Tom began to remember abuse, but it came back to him without the feelings. (Memories of abuse often surface initially like film clips. The pictures appear before the feelings are remembered and felt.) Now that he was in the second stage, he was healthy enough to experience the feelings attached with the events rather than recall them as if his memories were a movie about someone else.

In therapy, Tom looked at what was going on inside of him and walked through his feelings. By doing this he realized that he could tolerate the pain and the sadness. This was the beginning of a deepening process for him. These feelings did not have to destroy him, although he could have really destroyed his life by getting a divorce and reaching for a quick fix to a problem that had nothing to do with his wife. Had Tom not faced these feelings and instead had continued to try to suppress them, it is very likely that he would have ended up in relapse. By facing these feelings he started a healing process within himself which strengthened both his marriage and his sense of peace with himself in the long run.

When he was finally able to share what had happened in his childhood with his wife, she was able to understand him better and increase her compassion for him. They were in my office together when Tom told his wife about his abuse. Kim cried, because she now understood what was really going on inside of Tom and how ashamed and alone he felt. She walked over to the couch where Tom was sitting and held him against her breast as he cried for quite some time.

This couple is very close; they have one of the strongest marriages that I know of. By sharing and walking through their feelings, both separately and together, they are now truly intimate. They have a sense that they can face anything together.

Facing something inside ourselves and then changing it takes a lot of courage. Our society holds an attitude that if we change something in our outer lives by getting a divorce or moving or changing a job that this will cure the internal restlessness. It never does.

Reevaluating Friendship

Like many people in the second stage of healing, Sarah, whom we discussed in the chapter on Stage I, experienced a renewal of the meaning of friendship in her life. One of the reasons she started to feel more satisfied in her dating life in the second stage of recovery was that she was learning how to establish friendships with men. She was no longer feeling needy in relationships with men; she was content inside herself and had started to enjoy living on her own and being single.

Sarah happened to be involved in AA, and as a result she had a lot of experiences where, after an AA meeting, she would go out with a group of people for coffee. These occasions helped her learn how to be comfortable and sociable in a group setting without having any expectations, and this new, relaxed attitude helped her really appreciate people and accept them for who they were. As a result, she experienced more satisfaction in her relationships with men as she began to date again.

For a romantic relationship to succeed, people first need to learn to treat each other as friends. Many couples forget to do this and, as a result, begin to treat and talk to each other in a way that they never would their friends. Before the healing process occurs, and even into early recovery, friendship is often confused with dependency. As a result, people in these kinds of "friendships" feel very anxious because they are not sure if they are in a relationship out of neediness or real caring.

People in the second stage of healing are growing in their ability to make the distinction between relationships that feel healthy and support their sense of self and relationships that feel dependent and unhealthy. Some of the values that we place on friendship in our culture are misconstrued to mean someone who will cover up for others or forgive them unconditionally. This is not true friendship. Many people who are healing from emotional trauma have experienced love in their friend and family relationships, but have never really experienced the kind of acceptance found in true friendship. People often learn for the first time in their lives what it is to be accepted and what real friendship is when they enter into a healing process.

A friend is someone who will be honest—not someone who flatters and says something that sounds nice even if it's not true. A friend might let us experience the consequences of our behavior rather than make excuses for us when we are doing something that is destructive to ourselves or another person. Friends look at themselves honestly and take their own inventory using us as a mirror. A friend may be someone who is willing to be courageous enough to admit, "I'm not feeling very close to you right now," and in doing so create an opening in the discussion whereby an honest interchange can occur, increasing the possibility of more closeness in the future. A friend is someone who can be there to listen and offer support, accepting us as we are, not trying to make us into something different.

Being a friend is not the same thing as being a counselor. In being a counselor, a certain distance is implied in the relationship—a kind of interaction that is somewhat removed and not truly intimate. True friendship means that the people involved are equals. They have to let themselves be vulnerable in order to learn how to be friends. This is a great challenge for people who want to be helpers, because the helper role is one that includes tremendous control.

Avoiding the Critical Parent/Bad Child Syndrome

In some cases, marriages that begin prior to healing and in early recovery are based on the kind of helping role where one person is wounded and the other is the strong one. This could be called the critical parent/bad child syndrome because it is a phenomenon involving a person who runs the life of another person who is labeled as the person with the "problem," whether it is chemical dependency, depression, or some other kind of wound.

In recovery, both partners must heal. They must truly be equal. This can be painful to the person in the "parent" role because it means giving up a lot of control, which may represent a real danger to the person in control. Yet at the same time, many opportunities and benefits result from giving up this kind of control. One of the opportunities is that the relationship becomes more equal and therefore more fun for both partners. It is not much fun for one person to take on a parental role in a marriage. It is often very harmful to a healthy sex life. If people feel that they need to be in control all the time, they are not going to be relaxed enough to enjoy spontaneous, healthy, fun, loving relationships. This is one of the many reasons why it is important for couples to work on healing together.

Milestones in Deepening (Stage Two)

•You will renew and strengthen your commitment to your chosen path of recovery.

•You will continue to improve your physical health.

•You will identify secondary addictions and destructive behaviors that hold you back.

•You will identify boredom and find out what is underneath it.

•You will learn to forgive yourself for not being perfect.

•You will look inside yourself when you feel stuck.

•You will stop blaming others for internal problems.

•You will learn to identify and get support for intense feelings.

•You will learn to say "I don't know" or "I need time to think about that" rather than to answer questions before you are ready.

•You will learn to stop and think before taking impulsive action.

•You will identify old attitudes that are not working anymore.

•You will work on developing new attitudes and the behaviors that are consistent with them.

•You will learn to recognize, respect and honor your inner voice.

•You will notice a greater range of feeling than before.

•You will learn of the value of friendships and that friends are equals.

•You will learn that it is important to be a friend before a romantic relationship occurs.

•You will release any people you have attempted to control or manipulate.

Stage III in Healing and Recovery

Connectedness Corresponds to Adolescence

Connectedness is, simply, a joining together. If being connected involves joining two things together, one might ask what those two elements are that are joined together during the third stage of healing? Connectedness in our context refers to people who are now ready to connect with the outside world and feel like participants in the world, perhaps for the first time in their lives.

Dana is a woman who wrote the following description in her fifth year in recovery:

> I am in my fifth year of recovery and my life is like night and day compared to what it was. I am in a loving and fun relationship; we are married and completely committed. Miles now has a good job, we own our home, and best of all ,we have a beautiful baby. Life is a joy to me now. I am motivated by faith, not fear. And it just gets better.

That sounds pretty terrific. But what preceded this? Dana went on a journey to get to this fifth year and to the promise and the hope she feels. Who was Dana four, five, six years ago?

Dana is experiencing healing from a combination of things, including a horrendous childhood of physical abuse with two alcoholic parents. Her father disclosed that he was homosexual when Dana was eighteen; several years later he died of AIDS. She had two brothers, one of whom died of Leukemia; the other was born profoundly mentally retarded and was institutionalized.

During her teens, Dana developed a combination of eating disorders as a result of a modeling career that put pressure on her to keep her weight low. She developed bulimarexia, which is a combination of anorexia and bulimia; her eating cycle involving bingeing and purging food as well as compulsive exercising. Later on she discovered cocaine and speed as other tools to keep her weight down, and at this time she got involved in an obsessive relationship with Jerry, who was a cocaine dealer. This relationship lasted about three years; she became so depressed that she made two suicide attempts during this period.

When she first began therapy (as an ex-model) she weighed eighty-eight pounds and had not menstruated for five years. With intense psychotherapeutic work and high-quality medical consultation, she came up to a normal weight and normal physical health within about a year. She realized she was going to have to give up alcohol, cocaine, and other drugs to recover from her eating disorder—she could not afford to use any drugs that might throw off her natural sense of appetite. Like most recovering bulimics, she had to be very sure about when she was hungry or full; she could not afford to take any kind of chemicals that might disguise basic physical hunger and satiation. She began with tremendous emotional pain in therapy because she had lost most of the men in her life in one way or another, including her brothers, her father and her lover. Now she was losing the crutch of chemicals as well.

She wrote about what it was like for her in her twenties, before her recovery:

> "In 1977 I reached a point in my life when nothing seemed to be working. I couldn't fake it anymore. I wasn't fooling anybody, but regardless, I kept on acting.
>
> "In my early twenties I got deeper and deeper into bulimia,

alcoholism, and drug abuse. Without realizing it, I was drawn to men with drug problems. I was with Jerry for three years. It was a very abusive type of relationship, but in a silent way. There was no communication—there was only manipulation, dishonesty, and the withholding of feelings, affection, and sex. We never spoke of the self-abuse we recognized in each other. Each person's self-abuse justified the other's. We coexisted in a slowly dying state.

"When I moved on, my inner loneliness became more acute. I got involved with a coke addict/dealer. He reminded me of my dad; he was sometimes sweet, sometimes cold, but always inconsistent and noncommittal. This relationship had a lot of drama. It went on for three years and it was very painful. I then went through a year and a half of many men, all addicts or alcoholics. I was looking for a love, someone to save me. These actions brought my self-worth to a low point. I became more afraid and lonely and had thoughts of suicide.

"I realized that my first commitment was to my addictions. I felt desperately out of control. I reached a point when I could no longer go on with my half-existence. Finally I reached out for help."

Six months after Dana began her recovery process she met Miles, who was to become her husband. It was another year, during which they slowly developed a friendship, before they began to live together. Now Dana is almost eight years into her recovery. She and Miles have been married seven and a half years and are enjoying building a family.

Dana wrote about her recovery process and how this affected her budding relationship with Miles. He was using drugs when they met, but she felt he was different than the other men she had known. He recognized his problems and wanted to get well.

"We didn't jump into bed right away; we were friends for months before we became serious. We stayed up late at night talking and reading the AA Big Book. He became involved in AA and stopped using drugs. When we became more deeply

> involved, it was difficult for us both. His old life pulled at him. He was afraid of all the changes he was going through. He had a lot of guilt to contend with as well. When he made the commitment to be clean and sober, we went to AA meetings on a daily basis together. The twelve steps not only benefited our individual programs, but it was a working basis for our relationship as well. We grew to trust each other and to communicate in all respects. I have never felt so loved by another human being."

As I've mentioned, the process of learning to be friends has many benefits. One of those benefits may be that the basis of a strong friendship can lead to a love relationship like Miles and Dana's. Keep in mind, however, that Miles and Dana were willing to take some time to get to know one another. Healing happens slowly, although many milestones along the way let you know that you are making improvements and enriching your life in many different ways. In the same way, relationships can only be built when people go at their own pace. One cannot rush healing or friendship, just as one cannot rush the normal growth and maturation process. Here are the elements found in connectedness, the third stage of healing:

The Connection Between Sexuality and True Intimacy

The blossoming friendship that developed into a romantic relationship for Miles and Dana is another hallmark of third-stage recovery. Third stage recovery for single people usually involves a kind of "relationship readiness," which has a lot to do with the awareness that sexuality involves a lot more than the physical act. Miles and Dana were a little bit afraid of getting involved sexually because they knew that they had both experienced obsessive relationships in the past that were part of their drug and alcohol use. As a result, they took their time before getting physical.

People who have used sex in the past to keep from getting close in relationships are often particularly afraid of becoming physically involved while in the third stage of recovery. In a way, this is a healthy fear, because it is based on the knowledge that getting physically involved in a relationship involves a serious and deep commitment. There are many reasons to not rush into physical involvement; one of them has to do with physical health and the avoidance of disease. AIDS is a very real phenomenon, and the threat of sexually transmitted disease was something that Dana was acutely and painfully aware of, because her father had died of AIDS. She decided that it was important for her to wait until she was going to be truly ready to make an emotional commitment before letting herself become physically involved in a relationship. It is said that when we become sexually involved with another person that we become sexually involved with every person he or she has ever been involved with. This is a poignant truth, so it is vital that we reach a strong level of trust and candor before becoming physically involved.

In the past, when Dana would meet a man, she would go to bed with him quickly. Afterwards she would be uncomfortable with him; in many cases she did not want to see him again. Her behavior did not allow for closeness and comfort. She did things very differently with Miles, however, and discovered that they had a solid base of friendship and a strong comfort level with each other by the time they were ready to be physically close. As a result, the physical closeness built more emotional intimacy for the two of them, and they wanted to be together and savor their closeness after the sexual act.

Dealing with Secondary Issues

Another factor people often find in the third stage of recovery is the need and desire to deal with any secondary behavioral patterns they may identify in themselves. Some examples might be workaholism, gambling, overeating, smoking, casual sex, and other kinds of escapist activities like compulsive television watching and compulsive spending.

It is no accident that it can take several years for a person to be ready to deal with a strong secondary behavioral pattern. It is scary enough to deal with the primary self-destructive behavior, and it may take all the person's energy and commitment to deal with it honestly. Even thinking about dealing with something else often feels overwhelming in early recovery. In Stage II, people often identify secondary behaviors. In Stage III, they begin to deal with them, and begin a secondary healing process.

Being Honest About Who You Are

A lot of professional people deal with workaholism at the third stage of recovery. For example, I once counseled a physician named Bob who, like many other physicians, was a workaholic. He would spend a minimum of 120 hours a week working. He was a recovering adult child of an alcoholic and was involved in a children of alcoholics recovery program, psychotherapy, and bibliotherapy—he did a lot of reading on the subject.

During his third year of recovery, Bob had a disconcerting thing happen to him. He was sitting in the corner of a room waiting for a surgical conference to begin at the hospital where he admitted his patients. He was trying to be very low-key because he didn't want anybody to notice that he was reading a book about adult children of alcoholics. At that moment, a surgeon named Marsha walked up to him. Bob was an internist, and like most surgeons and internists, Marsha and Bob normally got along about as well as cats and dogs. However, on this particular day, Marsha smiled pleasantly and said, "What are you reading?" At this point, Bob blushed because he really didn't want to talk about his personal life with a surgeon. Unable to escape his predicament, he told her the truth and showed her the cover of the book. At this point, Marsha exclaimed, "Oh, are you an adult child of an alcoholic? So am I." They got into a conversation on their childhoods and how being an adult child of an alcoholic affected their adult lives and their intimate relationships. Subsequently, Marsha and Bob began dating, and now involved in an intimate relationship. Marsha and Bob have both reduced their work schedules quite a bit now that they are into the third stage of recovery together. When they discovered each other they also discovered the fact that they want to spend more time together and less of their time working. At the third stage of healing, people are often more comfortable with the recovery process and with themselves, and this is certainly true of Marsha and Bob. As a result, they have been able to stop working compulsively.

In early recovery, it can be too scary to cut down on the work schedule, particularly for professional people who have used work as a survival tool for most of their adult lives. By the third stage of recovery, however, most people have relaxed a little bit, are more comfortable with themselves in general, and are able to look out and appreciate the world. They want to slow down enough to do things other than work. As a result, this is a stage where a lot of the fun begins for people—the fun of just being alive and being human. It is not unusual to see people like Marsha and Bob take several months off and go on a trip around the world, go hiking in the Sierras, or do something on the same order. When people emerge as complete human beings they are ready to connect with the world.

Vulnerability and the Emotional Roller Coaster Ride

Another of the hallmarks of this third stage of recovery is the depth of joy (and sometimes the depth of misery) that people experience because their feelings are so exposed and they are so vulnerable at this point. Like adolescents, they often feel joys and pains intensely. They feel very alive and are open to a whole spectrum of emotions.

For instance, I have noticed that people who decide to give up the nicotine habit find many benefits at this stage, some of which are physical. But there are many emotional benefits as well. When people stop smoking they may become aware of the depth of their emotions in a relatively short time. It takes several months to detox from nicotine and the many other active chemicals present in cigarettes, and during those months, many people go on a journey of internal discovery. An acuity of the senses, particularly taste, helps them discover a lot of new things about themselves and, as a result, they begin to see a lot more color in the world and feel more alive. They may come out of a kind of haze that they had been hiding behind as a result of the nicotine habit. It is no small thing to give up a lifetime of coping through the use of a chemical like caffeine or nicotine, so it is not that surprising that those who do find new and intense emotions in the third stage.

Unfortunately, people who have stopped using alcohol or another drug commonly discover at this stage that they have a secondary eating problem. This could be compulsive eating or some other type of eating disorder including compulsive sugar consumption. People can deal with eating disorders by enrolling in programs such as Overeaters Anonymous; books and self-help groups can provide support as well. Perhaps best of all, the same healing process and its milestones apply to secondary issues as they do to primary ones.

By the third stage of recovery, people have learned a lot about the recovery process and about how to substitute healthy behaviors for unhealthy ones. As a result, they are in a good position to stop harmful secondary behavior patterns and to replace them with healthier behaviors. It is one of the miracles of life that we become aware of problems in life at about the same time we become aware of the tools to deal with the problems. People in the third stage of recovery have so many tools already at their disposal to deal with self-destructive behavior that they are in a particularly strong position.

But how does dealing with a secondary issue affect relationships? Obviously, a secondary addiction can affect a person's ability to relate to another person. Take workaholism, for example. It is very difficult to get close to someone who is working 120 hours a week, and the survival skill of compulsive working is usually developed by people who grew up feeling very alone and who work as a way to survive the pain of feeling so alone. In this case, it is important to replace the work with something else, and to learn more about having fun and healthy play. Many people who never learned how to play as children were busy acting like adults and running families when they were young. It is imperative for those people to learn how to play and relax at this stage of recovery.

Emergence of the Invisible

Many people make a decision in childhood to be invisible to survive. Some of these people try to escape from life in other ways later on in their lives. This results from the decision to be invisible as a child to avoid pain and fear.

For example, Tom, who was discussed in an earlier chapter, was sexually abused by his mother as a little boy. He made his decision to be invisible at four years of age. As a matter of fact, the figure he identified with most at the time was Casper the Friendly Ghost. (Some of you may remember this children's cartoon which first ran during the early fifties.) A child who is experiencing terror may often decide to be invisible, a fly on the wall, a ghost, or some other benign force that can see everything that is going on and yet not be seen by others. Some people can practically blend into the walls so that others do not notice their physical presence.

Being such a person has obvious appeal for a child who lives in fear. However, people who adopt this survival mechanism often find that it causes problems in later life when they want to be in relationships. A person cannot be emotionally present and invisible at the same time.

Being involved in an intimate relationship involves being seen and truly known. If a person has at some point made a decision to be invisible, he or she will find it difficult to achieve that kind of intimacy. The good news is that just being aware that you made a decision like that in the past is a very powerful tool to begin gradually to let yourself notice times when you are being invisible. Talking about it and acknowledging that this is an issue for you can be very helpful.

Being invisible certainly had its positive qualities for Tom as a child, and he found advantages to it as an adult. Because he knew how to be invisible, he could choose to be so when he wished. For example, Tom lived in Manhattan for many years and he was never mugged, robbed, or victimized by a violent act. He attributed this fact to his ability to be invisible—he felt he had a kind of imaginary shield around him. People simply didn't notice him on subways or on the street, and he felt he was never the victim of violent acts because nobody even noticed him. Such a skill could be viewed as a positive thing in a large city.

However, what if, like Tom, you started to go to support group early in your healing process? You would need to be noticed sometimes, because you would need to learn to reach out for support. That support would be very hard to reach out for because you were used to being invisible. This was a problem for Tom in his early sobriety. He had to learn gradually to let himself be more visible at AA meetings, to raise his hand sometimes and talk. He struggled with this at first, but the risk carried many benefits. Eventually, Tom got to pick and choose the times when he would be invisible instead of letting his childhood decision rule him. He began to choose the times when he would be invisible and the times when he would be known, and found himself opting for the latter more and more.

Connecting With The World

One of the themes of the third to the fifth year in recovery is the reconnection with the world. By the time people enter the third stage of recovery, they have worked on themselves to the degree that they are a lot healthier and at more peace with themselves. As a result, they tend to attract healthier people. They then begin to establish healthier relationships and connect with people who have a high degree of self-esteem.

This is a good time for people experiencing the healing process to branch out and get to know people who are not involved in programs of recovery and who have other things to offer in a friendship. By the time people reach the third stage of recovery, they are generally at a sufficient level of health to recognize health when they see it. Socializing with people from all kinds of backgrounds is beneficial for those in the healing process. It is good for single people who want to learn about being in a healthy romantic relationship may want to socialize with couples who can act as role models of what a healthy relationship is like.

As Dana entered the third year of her healing process, she became more interested in hiking and backpacking. This opened up a new world for her. She got involved with a group of people who went on regular backpacking trips to the mountains. Many of these people had never had experience with chemical dependency in their lives, and had always had a fairly healthy lifestyles. As a result, they had another perspective on life to offer Dana. She came to realize that she could be friends with many people who are basically good, healthy human beings. She learned a lot from her experiences with this group and began to realize that she did not have to have crisis in her life in order to stay interested and excited about living. She learned that some of the subtle things in life are among the most important. She learned to appreciate the peace and the quiet in the simplicity of nature, and how to share that with other people. She also learned that she did not need to experience pain in order to remind herself that she existed.

Even when people experience some strong emotions in the third stage as a result of increased memory recall of their early lives and the increased ability to feel, they still experience a kind of deep inner peace. Emotions no longer rule the person at a deep level. In Stage III, people learn to feel their emotions, but not to act on every emotion. That distinction is an important part of the natural maturation process as well as the process of healing.

The Grief Process and Life Experience

Dana experienced a grief process during her third stage of recovery as a result of her father's death from AIDS. But she was able to feel the feelings—not be overwhelmed by them—and did not go back to numbing herself through the use of a chemical or food. This was because she had developed a deep sense of spiritual peace that helped her cope with the intense feelings; she could felt a sense of inner peace that had been built as a result of all the work she had done on herself in the previous stages. Now she had a sense of contact with herself, and she knew that she was never alone. She could handle any feelings that emerged.

The grief process that arises as a result of experiencing a loss like Dana's loss of her father contains in it every emotion known to human beings. Dana experienced all of the emotions that are a normal part of the grief process, yet a part of her stood back and appreciated the depth and the texture of emotions that she could feel now that she was in her third stage. The richness to her life in the third stage stayed with her, so that life became less like a one-dimensional picture and more like a multidimensional sculpture she could walk around and feel the texture of; she could appreciate all the subtlety and the depth inherent in the life experience.

This new sense of depth and meaning experienced in the third stage of recovery makes way for the opening of the heart, which is essential for the development of compassion to occur. True compassion begins during this stage when people begin to realize that they have something to give, and that they do not need to receive in return. They are not needy nor dependent anymore.

If they are single, they feel more complete within themselves. Those who are in a relationship or who want to be in one are seeking a deep and balanced adult-to-adult committed relationship and all the work and benefits that this entails. So at this stage, the strong and broad range of emotions that are felt are tempered by increased spiritual depth; people develop a sense that they are not merely surviving, but can grow richer as a result of the spiritual lessons that they learn from life. This is what Dana did.

The sense of connectedness that occurs in the third stage of recovery is a deep feeling that pervades the whole life of a person, both internally and externally. Because individuals are more connected with themselves internally, they are more connected to certain aspects of the outer world that they may have felt alienated from in the past. They experience a sense of really belonging and a renewed sense of joy in being human and being part of the world.

This sense of exploring life and connecting with it is similar, in a developmental way, to adolescence. At both stages, people are developing a strong sense of identity. And in both cases, it is a big task. The opportunity for growth is great; the danger is that sometimes people can feel that they are on an emotional roller coaster and may need to be reminded that nothing lasts forever.

Strong emotions come and go. *Emotions do not require action.* Change is the order of the day in this stage of healing, just as it is during adolescence.

•You will learn that you do not need to take action on every feeling or thought.

•You will learn to be friends before being lovers.

•You will learn the connection between compassion and forgiveness, starting with yourself.

•You will learn the difference between secrecy and privacy.

•You will learn to reduce the number and the power of the secrets in your life.

•You will learn to identify fear and deal with it in a productive way.

•You will learn to let go of resentments that are hurting you.

•You will learn to express feelings at the time an event occurs rather than seventy-two hours to twenty years later.

•You will experience healthy self-pride.

•You will learn to get involved in a relationship out of mutual interest and caring for another person rather than out of pity for them.

•You will learn from the past and not get stuck in it.

•You will recapture innocence.

•You will learn to listen.

•You will feel joy.

•You will learn to respect your body and its messages.

•You will make a commitment to deal with secondary addic tions and destructive behaviors.

•You will learn that you are the master of your emotions and that their intensity does not have to control you.

Stage IV in Healing and Recovery

Integration Corresponds with Initiation into Adulthood

Integration is feeling whole or complete, and is the result of the work done in the first three stages. There are many benefits, some obvious and some more subtle. The sense of internal wholeness or completion can feel like receiving a laurel wreath after winning a particularly challenging game. Sometimes, however, feeling whole can be at odds with a person's environment and lifestyle.

When Jack began therapy with me he had been in the process of healing for eight years. He was a survivor of childhood incest, and at this stage his feelings were mixed. He had worked very hard on his path of healing, but now he was approaching something which felt like a midlife crisis at age thirty-five. (Stage IV can often feel like a midlife crisis regardless of the chronological age of the person, because this stage is analogous to the gateway to adulthood.)

In Jack's case, he had done a lot of healing already—enough to know that his current life was at odds with who he really felt he was inside. He was a strapping six-foot three, two hundred pound man, well dressed in a three-piece suit that was appropriate for his job as an investment banker. Although he showed all outward signs of success and stability, he felt that he was being spiritually and emotionally strangled. As he talked, he proceeded to loosen and then take off his tie, as if it would literally strangle him.

He was quickly coming to the realization that he was and always had been gay. He also was a sculptor, and wanted to pursue this as a full-time career. The problem was that Jack was married and the father of a beautiful little girl whom he loved. His wife had no idea that he was gay.

The values that he had developed in his healing process included honesty at all costs; he could not justify leading a double life anymore. While never passionate, his was a friendly marriage—he truly liked his wife as a friend. However, he maintained a close, long-term lover with whom he wanted to live. The stress of feeling one way and living another was getting to him. His blood pressure was up and he was experiencing frequent violent nightmares where he was being chased by faceless, shadowy, frightful creatures.

Jack's problem, although particularly dramatic, is representative of the kind of realizations people have in Stage IV recovery. People learn they must be authentic. *This means that their lifestyle must match who they know they are inside, or they experience great stress.* Jack eventually left his wife. His life settled down, and after an initial crisis period, things worked out well for him. He now has joint custody with his ex-wife and his daughter has made the adjustment.

It was a rough first year, however, after he announced to his wife that he was gay. As well as dealing with the divorce, he quit his job to become a full-time artist and had to cope with financial insecurity. But because he knew what was right for him, he made his choices and has not looked back.

Many people go through major relationship and work changes in Stage IV. One of the dangers is that people may not feel they can compromise anymore. However, when it comes to being true to oneself, this refusal to compromise is also one of the opportunities. The benefits of honesty with oneself include inner peace and true joy.

Self-Honesty and Accelerated Emotional Growth

A deep level of self-honesty is required to be at peace. When the

Russian writer, Leo Tolstoy, was facing midlife, he plunged into a serious depression. As a matter of fact, he felt that his life was "broken," that something had changed deep within him and that his deep desire to live was matched by a deep desire not to live. He was so depressed that he didn't have enough energy to do anything. He was frozen, unable to take any action.

Tolstoy passed through his personal crisis in the same way that many other people get through the challenges of the stage of Integration. But merely "getting through" life may not seem to be an acceptable answer during this stage. As I've explained, the stages of healing parallel normal emotional growth and development, and the fourth stage is very much like midlife. Some people have an experience similar to Tolstoy's during fourth stage of recovery, regardless of their chronological age or background. Something about the recovery process in and of itself accelerates growth and development. After people have caught up to their chronological age in terms of growth and development in early recovery, they go beyond that and begin to experience a depth and freedom in terms of exploring the self.

During this stage of the healing process (and during midlife crisis), people have basically two choices. They can become rigid and old very quickly, or they can risk change and remain open to whatever life has to offer them.

Fourth-Stage Complacency

One of the blessings and dangers of fourth-stage healing is that people become self-confident in their ability to understand certain fundamentals about their recovery and in their knowledge of the basic tools of healing. Complacency can sometimes set in and the recovery process can become automatic—people stop thinking about what healing really means to them. Instead of becoming complacent, however, they can choose to recommit to healing and the changes it entails.

Human beings are dynamic, not static. If we do not choose growth, change may occur anyway in the form of crisis or illness.

The need to grow and change does not go away; sometimes negative changes become more dramatic if needs are not attended to. Physical illnesses, accidents, or other kinds of tragedies demand attention. We cannot turn away—we can no longer turn a blind eye or a deaf ear to the message being sent. We can choose to change, as Jack did, or else change may find us.

Of course, knowing what we need to do is not the same as actually following through and doing that thing. In the case of Jeff, a lawyer who eventually left his practice to sail around the world, there were things that he had promised to himself he would do during his youth. Sailing around the world happened to be one of those things. But making the commitment to fulfilling his dream meant shaking up his life in a lot of ways. He had a comfortable lifestyle, so this was not easy for him. Many times the questions faced during Stage IV require shaking up old patterns.

Being True to the Self

By the fourth stage, people in the healing process have done a lot of fine tuning in terms of their dialogue with their internal selves. As a result, they can't get away with as much dishonesty or lack of self-integrity as they could earlier in their program. Part of this is just a function of being more aware of themselves, but part of it is the result of a greater degree of spiritual awareness that occurs during the fourth stage—it does not allow for a lot of self-delusion. The inner voice comes across loud and clear and can be a guide for the person when they begin to ask questions like, "What is the purpose of my life?" and "What is the meaning of my life?" This is a wonderful time to begin a journal, to do dream work, deep analytic work, and/or somatic work, including body therapies and massage, which can help release deep-seated feelings.

Many ironies and conundrums come about in the fourth-stage healing process. One of the ironies is that people who are in the fourth stage have achieved so much inner health by this time that they quickly recognize when they are feeling less than integrated or whole. Sometimes people in the fourth stage talk about feeling chaotic inside while, in fact, they have simply become more aware of things they would not have noticed one or two years before. They will not settle for half a life as they may have before they are willing to experience the discomfort of change in order to reap the benefits. They know that the self cannot be put aside.

If we do not attend to the needs of the self, then the messages telling us to do so become larger and more dramatic with time.

There was a play upon which a popular movie was based a few years ago, called *The Little Shop of Horrors.* Although there were human actors, the real star of the show was a plant that became larger and larger, finally growing to the point that it was bursting out of the store. It constantly screamed, "feed me, feed me, feed me!" The self, if it is not attended to, is a lot like that plant. It will grow larger, screaming to be fed. What nourishes the self is the food of the spirit and the soul.

The self speaks to us in a variety of ways: first in little ways, and, if we don't attend to it, in larger and larger ways. Dreams and meditation are two of the primary ways the self speaks to us. Dreams are discussed later on in this book. All we have to do is learn to listen and follow the guidance provided.

The Self, the Creative Process, and Freedom of Choice

If people do not attend to the early messages in Stage IV of the healing process, sometimes they may disrupt their lives in ways such as getting a divorce or having an affair in a misguided attempt to try to ease the need for intense inner growth. However, changing something in their outer world may not be helpful. A person must sort out genuine needs for change before acting.

One of the major dangers of the fourth stage of healing is that the person may try to stop this growth process by relapsing and going back to destructive behaviors. But the growth process will not go away; it must be faced. It is one of the most exciting times in life and, although it may seem ironic to a person in stage four, it is one of the most freeing. For people who have lived their lives as a series of "shoulds" and "ought tos," this is a period of time when they can release themselves from those false obligations and really find out what they want and be guided by an inner drive. In short, they can put aside the expectations of the world.

This is a very liberating experience; many artists and writers do their most creative work during the stage of integration. It is a great time to go into depth in psychotherapy, because people are stable enough to know how to deal with any anxious feelings that might come up. They are, in general, better able to deal with their inner feelings and do deep insight-oriented work. It is a very rich time internally.

At the integration stage of healing, some people also first become aware that they truly have a choice concerning whether or not they want to be in a relationship. Because they have done so much work on themselves, they are less likely to come into or maintain a relationship with another human being merely out of need. If they choose to be in a relationship, they are ready to enter into it with a true ability to share.

When people describe the onset and development of relationships that occur at this point in recovery, they often say that they were "ready to receive love." People who are ready to receive love are also ready to give love. Early in the healing process, people often think of themselves as able to give love, and yet they often see themselves as not being the recipient of love. By fourth stage of recovery, people realize they cannot truly give love without receiving it, and vice versa. Giving and receiving becomes like two hands clasped and interlocked.

People at this stage do continue to identify the barriers that may keep them from experiencing a sense of wholeness, and continue to deal with them. But the primary barriers are gone. People who have maintained continued sobriety, for instance, usually do not experience urges to use drugs or alcohol, and deal with other issues besides abstinence alone as they arise.

Celebration of Life

The real payoff for people who attend to the needs that we discussed earlier in the four stages of healing is the feeling of renewal and celebration of life. For instance, when Jeff got up the courage to tell his wife that he wanted to sail around the world, she surprised him by saying that she wanted to go with him. They had a terrific time, and he ended up feeling a great sense of renewal in his life. They had another child and created a whole new family in their early forties. As individuals and as a couple they were willing to take the risks and challenges that are presented at this stage of integration. They are a happy couple and have the benefits of being parents a second time around, with all of the confidence and knowledge of their earlier parenting experience.

There are many ways to celebrate life at this fourth stage, just as there are at midlife. Making a healthy break with the past, taking a healthy, appropriate risk, starting a new family, renewing an old relationship or starting a new one, starting a new career, getting deeply involved in a spiritual program, finding new creative expression are some of them. These are all examples of the kind of joy and adventure presented in the fourth stage of healing for those who want to take the risk and continue to grow.

Being a Victim is not the Same as Being a Survivor

A psychotherapist who is a second generation holocaust survivor and who recently survived a devastating fire that destroyed his home shared the following perspective on being a survivor:

Immediately after the fire, his and the other families whose homes were destroyed were presented with red cards that had the word "VICTIM" printed on them in large letters. The identification cards were to be presented to stores so that merchants could give a discount on goods to fire victims.

Every time this man and his family members presented the card, they received a rush of emotional support and sympathy and were asked to recount their story. After a while, however, my friend came to the conclusion that he had passed the victim stage and did not want to continue recounting the story of the trauma. While remaining a victim was somewhat appealing because of the sympathy it engendered, he realized that he and his family needed to move past this in order to be survivors. They held a family meeting to discuss the matter and concluded that the time to be victims was past. They agreed that when presenting the card they would characterize themselves as survivors, cutting short descriptions of the fire. They would thank the merchants for their support and move on.

This story illustrates that there is a time to be a victim—early in recovery. To stay a victim, however, is to remain in a childlike position and never to grow up. The fourth stage of healing is about growing up.

Taking adult responsibility for moving on and living a fulfilling life can be painful at first. However, the sympathy in the eyes of people responding to the victim is replaced with respect and understanding of the need to move on. Self-esteem increases as people take adult responsibility, and this new-found self-respect radiates out to others in our families and our communities. People begin to believe that the figure looking back at them in their mirror every day is truly an adult human being and not a forty-year-old body masking a crouching, terrorized child underneath. The freedom of truly feeling like an adult who has choices is worth any discomfort experienced in giving up the victim role.

This completes my description of the growth process during the various stages of healing. Once again, I would like to emphasize that by no means are these stages cast in concrete. People go at their own pace; they experience healing in ways that are unique to them. That is part of the joy of discovery which is, in turn, part of the healing. These stages are intended as guidelines only, and as a way to observe and acknowledge progress.

Naturally, growth and healing never end, and life constantly offers challenges. Sometimes it throws in a crisis or two. There is no panacea which prevents change, crisis, or pain. By the same token, however, people learn by the end of the fourth stage of healing that they will get through whatever life presents with grace, dignity, support and love. That knowledge brings a person far beyond mere survival. It affords people opportunities to soar beyond any wounds they have received and to experience the fullness of life's journey.

•You will break the chain of hopelessness, shame and secrecy that may have been handed down from generation to generation in your family.

•You will learn to validate yourself.

•You will experience freedom from self-pity.

•You will experience the self and live in harmony with that experience.

•You will learn to give as well as to receive in a relationship.

•You will experience a deep sense of inner peace and joy even during times of crisis.

•You will learn how to choose a partner who is right for you.

•You will find that you are creative and express this creativity.

•You will see choice in your life.

•You will feel as if you belong.

•You will have fun and know how to relax.

•You will find a deep sense of purpose to your life.

•You will want become more interested in being of service to others.

•You will care about the consequences of your actions on others.

•You will begin to think about the legacy this generation leaves for the next.

•You will become more interested in connecting with your community.

•You will seek a sense of connection to your ethnocultural or family heritage.

Relapse Prevention

John's experiences are living proof to me that behavioral dependency can be every bit as destructive as an addiction to chemicals. They also confirm that there is a natural, predictable course of healing that applies to all recovery regardless of the wound. In this chapter, John's story will be used to illustrate the dangers of relapse. Tools for relapse avoidance that are useful in dealing with all destructive behaviors will then be presented—including but not limited to:

- Chemical addictions (including prescription and non-prescription drugs)
- Compulsive behaviors around sex and love
- Compulsive spending
- Compulsive worrying and mental obsessing
- Compulsive working and busyness

John is a successful software developer for a large Silicon Valley computer firm. He is single, in his mid-thirties, and has a graduate-level education and a high yearly income. He could be the envy of many people, but his increasing material success was, in a way, part of his problem. The more successful he became, the more empty he felt inside. In time he developed two serious compulsions, one of which was life-threatening.

Here is John's story in his own words:

My name is John. This is a story about sex compulsion and recovery.

I think my sex compulsion started when I was an infant. My mother seldom held me and seldom allowed others to. I remember climbing on people and asking for hugs. My mother sometimes joked that she hoped I would marry someone affectionate, because I seemed to need a lot of affection. As a teenager and a young man, I remember yearning for physical affection seeing little hope of ever getting it. The yearning became an obsession. It wasn't until years later that I found an outlet for that obsession.

For many years I traveled back and forth to San Francisco, and I always passed by the strip clubs on Broadway. I never went in, but I was always curious as to what they were like. Finally, one night, during a particularly stressful period of my life, I went in. This began a pattern of acting out that was to go on for many years. The pattern went something like this:

First would come the thoughts. I could get high just thinking about acting out. Sometimes I would feel chilled, or feel a knot in my throat. Then my thoughts would lock onto acting out. Soon I would reach a point of no return. No matter what anyone said or did, it was only a matter of time before I acted out.

The next step was to go to an Automated Teller Machine and withdraw one to two hundred dollars from my savings account. Then I would go to San Francisco and go to a club. I liked clubs that had so-called "lap dancing." This is where the strippers, after performing, would come into the audience and sit on customers' laps in exchange for tips. Although I call this a sex compulsion, my main reason for doing this was not to have sex, but just to have someone hold me. The only problem was that once I started, I couldn't stop. The more I tipped, the longer they would stay, or the more they would let me touch them. And the more I acted out, the more I wanted. I sometimes stayed until the place closed or until I ran out of money. That meant staying until 2:00 AM or spending all of the one or two hundred dollars that I had. But I also paid in terms of health. If I stayed out late, I would often be tired or ill for the next few days.

The women who sat with me were very good at what they did. Perhaps because they had been abused themselves they knew how to make me feel good. They made me feel like I was handsome, interesting, and very special to them. Most of all, they gave me the physical affection that I hungered for and didn't get much of as a child.

Sometimes one of the women would say, "Wanna have some fun?" or, "I can show you a really good time," or "We can go somewhere else." Eventually I caught on that I could ask, too. I would often say, "Do you want to go out?" or, "I'd like to take you home." Even if she said no, I got high just from asking. If she said yes, then we would set up a meeting place near the club. I would leave and wait, sometimes an hour or more, for her to show up. Then we would meet and take a circuitous route to my car. (Though I didn't realize it at the time, this was one of the most dangerous parts of what I did. These clubs were in rough sections of town. While walking to my car, we would often go through deserted streets and dark alleys. The few people who were around looked like drug addicts, pushers, and street people. I am not very physically strong; I'm lucky that I was never attacked or robbed.)

I've always been terrified of catching a sexually transmitted disease, so even with the strippers I was very careful. I never touched their mouth or genitals or let them touch mine. But I often came very close, and after each encounter, I spent the next several weeks obsessing over whether or not I had 'slipped up.' Suppose I had touched her, suppose she touched me, even for just a second? I found myself compulsively reading everything I could on STDs, and compulsively checking my mouth and genitals for signs of disease. I remember once getting a small sore on my lip. It was just a harmless pimple, but until I found out for sure, I was in a deep depression, certain that I had caught something. After each episode I would swear to myself many times over, If only I have escaped injury this time, I will always be happy and never act out again.

Sometimes I did go for several months without acting out. During some of these periods, I didn't even have the desire. I thought I was free. I learned later that these times were only the downturns in my "cycle." The cycle lasted about two months, and after the downturn would come another period of acting out.

One of the most difficult parts of my compulsion was the shame and secrecy. I was very careful to hide what I was doing from everyone. While walking to the club, I would walk facing away from the street so that no one would recognize me. Before going in, I would glance around to make sure no one could see me. As far as I knew, none of my friends had any idea that I did this. Most of them would be shocked, if they could even believe it.

Where am I now? Except for one slip, it has been almost a year since I acted out. Many things have helped me to break free. First, I shared my addiction with my therapist. I'm not sure when I would have told her, but it happened when she asked me to tell her about my dark side—this addiction was and still is my darkest secret.

It was also around this time that I accepted that I was compulsive. Although I had never had a drinking or drug problem, I realized that, in a way, I was no different from someone who did. Secondly, I confronted an image of my mother (not my real mother) about her lack of affection. I did this in the presence of other men and shared my secret with them. That was difficult. I had to find men that I was certain I could trust, men who would understand, who would not judge me, and who would support me. Finally I started regularly attending support group meetings.

I identified the conditions under which I tended to act out. These were my cues: feeling lonely, feeling angry, being apart from friends, having a lot of idle time on my hands, having problems in my love life, and having stress at work. Whenever any of these conditions are present, I make an extra effort to keep in contact with my friends, especially those in the group.

> The greatest lesson that I have learned is that I am not alone. There are many others who have been where I am and who can show me the path to recovery, as I hope to show those who are now where I was.

John's story illustrates a number of points about the nature of compulsive behavior. One is that it has a predictable course: it grows worse with time. Unless there is a change like the perceptual shift I discussed in the section on Stage I recovery, things go downhill. However, healing also has a natural and predictable course. There are points along the path when a person's susceptibility to relapse (a return to the old lifestyle) is more probable than others.

Vulnerable Periods

Temptation is greater at some points than others. As in John's case, many of these can be noted ahead of time. Knowing when these times are empowers a person, and it behooves that person to plan ahead as much as possible. Some of the vulnerable points along the path are:

The First Ninety Days Most relapses occur during this time. That is why twelve-step programs emphasize daily contact with the program during the first three months. The old saying, "Ninety meetings in ninety days," is no accident. Whatever path a person chooses, concentrating one hundred percent on that path with a commitment to daily work through the first ninety days is essential.

Anniversaries Six months, one year and other anniversaries of starting a new life are often vulnerable points. It is important for people to remind themselves of these dates ahead of time so that they don't forget what life was like before they chose a healing, positive path. They may also want to focus on healing as a one-day-at-a-time phenomenon. Birthdays are important, but focusing on today is more important.

Times of Emotional Upheaval and Change During Stage III (Connectedness) During Stage III, people often hit an emotional bottom. Pain may be felt with particular intensity. They may be tempted to numb the pain, strong feelings, and memories which arise at this time. This is the stage when people most often need outside support in the form of counseling to learn about their own emotions.

During Stage IV—Integration During the fourth stage of healing, people face the need for lifestyle change that supports who they are at a deeper level. Some make these changes, but others resist them. The ones who resist them are often left with a gnawing feeling of discomfort within themselves. These people are at high risk for relapse unless they take an honest look at themselves and make the needed changes.

Taking Action to Prevent Relapse Knowing the susceptible times for relapse is helpful in and of itself, but action can be taken to follow up on this knowledge. Action is what really counts in the long run. Here are some strategies and tools that can prevent relapse:

Strengthening Supports All the supports mentioned in the section on Stage I are essential. Staying on the path when life produces challenges involves constant reminders to continue with the supports that work over time. Here is a formula to follow:

Supports must be equal to or greater than stressors in order to stay on the path. If the stress level is equal to or greater than the number and strength of the supports, relapse is a real possibility. People can make a list of supports and rate how strong they are on one side of a page and list stressors on the other; that way they can see how the situation stacks up, and which supports they will need.

The Behavioral Risk Scale

The Behavioral Risk Scale, or B.R.S., is a tool I developed over twenty years of research in the area of relapse prevention. Gradually, I noted that this scale applied to many destructive behavior patterns. Thousands of people have used it all over the world, and have found it easy to use.

Let us take a closer look at the scale and how it works to rate the factors that increase the probability of relapse. These factors are called cues. Thoughts, things, people, places, events and moods are all potential cues.

The Behavioral Risk Scale is a numerical scale from one to ten that you can picture in your mind.

1	2	3	4	5	6	7	8	9	10
No risk			Low risk			High risk			Relapse

Use it to chart the level of risk for each cue, and then add them up. Any total above five presents too great a risk. Let's take John's case as an example. He was engaged in two patterns of destructive behavior. One was compulsive spending; the second was going to strip joints (sexual compulsion).

The following were his cues:

- •the end of a two-month cycle of not acting out
- •driving to San Francisco
- •having over one hundred dollars of cash in pocket
- •feeling the need for affection
- •anger and/or frustration

No one of these factors alone was enough for him to act out, but several in combination placed him well above a five on the risk scale, which put him at high risk. Therefore on a day when he felt lonely, had cash, and had a reason to be near San Francisco, his rating on the risk scale was much too high. He had to reduce his risk factors individually to reduce his composite risk below five. By planning ahead, he learned to do exactly that. As a result, he maintained abstinence from his compulsions.

Here is an example of a man who had a chemical addiction, and how the scale worked for him:

Paul was about to get married, and his buddies were throwing a bachelor party for him. He used the scale and determined that the party put him at a risk of about ten, so he took action to reduce his risk.

First, he called the host and told him he didn't want anybody to bring drugs to the party. Second, he made a commitment not to drink alcohol at this party. The risk was reduced to about a five, which he found acceptable. He was able to attend the party, have a good time, and avoid relapse.

The few minutes spent considering a situation before taking action reduce risk because you are structuring the situation ahead of time. So buy some time for yourself by using the behavioral risk scale. Make a list of people, places, things, events and moods that increase risk of relapse, carry the image of it with you mentally, and plot the risk for any new situation.

Trance and Recovery I developed another tool that you can combine with the B.R.S. I call it Psychophysiological Re-Education (P.R.E), and it involves self-induced trance. It is a powerful tool. Here is a story that illustrates the role that P.R.E. can play in recovery:

Josh is an attorney who made an excellent recovery from his cocaine addiction over a fifteen-month period. Josh was a freebaser of cocaine, and had spent several hundred thousand dollars on his addiction. He came into therapy for an evaluation; the therapist recommended that he go into a thirty-day inpatient hospital program, which he did. He followed up with intensive therapy after being discharged; he also attended an anonymous twelve step group. These were the keys to his recovery.

One interesting angle to Josh's story, however, is that he, like many people addicted to drugs, had spent a good part of his life in a trance, which was part of his cycle of drug use. He found it helpful to examine how he experienced this trance, and to actually use a trance state as a way to help him in his recovery.

If Josh had had a tough day at the office, he would go out to lunch with a friend of his who was also a lawyer. They would have one or two beers with their meal (which was significant, because even small amounts of alcohol can set people up to want other drugs). After having the beer, Josh and his friend would often decide to go over to their dealer's house, buy some cocaine, and freebase it. Josh had difficulty remembering exactly what had happened on those occasions that led him to freebase cocaine. His lack of memory had to do with him being in a kind of trance from the time he sat down in the restaurant.

In a state of trance, the mind is focused on or narrowed to only one thing. Josh already had the idea in his mind that he wanted to do cocaine before he even sat down to lunch, so his mind was focused on it. The focus was to the extent that Josh was in a trance state. In this trance, Josh would get up, go to the phone, and dial his dealer's number automatically, so that he did not even think about it. (The reflex nature of one's actions is a good tip-off in determining a trance state.) After dialing the number, he would go with his friend to the dealer's house.

Josh still does not remember any of these trips, because he was "on automatic" at the time. Many of us have had the experience of road hypnosis, where we get into the car and make all the right moves to get to work without thinking about it. Often we remember getting into the car and arriving at the destination, but nothing between. This is a common example of a trance state in everyday life.

As part of his recovery process, Josh learned to recognize when he was in his trance state, and how to redirect it. He learned that because of a combination of factors, including the trance state and his conditioning, he had to avoid some situations, such as being in the restaurants where he and his friend used to meet. He was conditioned to think about cocaine when he was in those restaurants, so going to these places was a poor idea for him no matter why or with whom he went. (His conditioning might also have included hearing his friend's name or the name of a bar—any cue that would set off his drug urge.)

Josh learned that he could change his desire for drugs by changing his mental and physiological state with the technique P.R.E. (Psychophysiological Re-Education). When his mind would stray to thoughts like "Wouldn't some cocaine be great?" he recalled the feeling that went along with cocaine use: "I remember—it was a rush feeling and I liked it." Then would come drug desire, or thoughts like, "I'd like to try some now." At that point a physical change takes place in the body called "drug hunger," where the body actually begins to behave as if it were already under the influence of the drug when in fact the drug hasn't been taken. By then, most people are on the phone to their dealer. (In the case of cocaine, for example, the signs of this condition include an increased pulse rate, a dry mouth, changes in the pupils, a feeling of energy or euphoria, and sometimes sexual excitement.) The final step after drug hunger is actually taking the drug, causing a chemical change in behavior. So we follow the cycle from a thought to a feeling, to drug desire, to drug hunger, and finally to drug abuse.

P.R.E. takes into account that the most effective to stop this chain of events is at the thought stage. In other words, when the thought, "Wouldn't some cocaine be great," comes into the mind, it is important to stop the process before it goes further. This can be done by learning how to put oneself into a very relaxed state of being. This takes practice, but can be achieved by anyone.

A person might sit down in a comfortable chair, do some deep, slow breathing, and think about something relaxing—perhaps a vacation, or just lying in the sun. The idea is to conjure a mental scene that is visual, auditory, or both—as long as it leads to relaxation. The pulse rate goes down when a person begins to feel relaxed, decreasing by as much as ten to fifty beats per minute. This is an important point, because if the mind, just by thinking of a relaxing situation, can reduce your pulse rate, that shows the profound effect your mental state has on the body and the way it responds physically. As Josh discovered, when your pulse rate is lower and you are feeling relaxed, it is impossible to have an urge for a drug like cocaine.

Practice this relaxation exercise frequently during the day so that you train yourself to become relaxed quickly, deeply, and effectively. Relaxing is a skill that can be learned with practice. Whenever you find yourself thinking about a compulsion, relax immediately. Make your breathing deeper and slower, think about a relaxing situation or place, and reduce your pulse rate.

You can use P.R.E. anywhere along the thought, feeling, urge, and behavior chain, but it is easiest to do so at the beginning—the thought stage. By practicing the technique and implementing it quickly, you can save yourself a lot of torment and anguish. Josh found that he could stop having urges by using this technique, and the number of urges decreased every day until he had absolutely no urges to do cocaine. The number of thoughts he had about cocaine per day diminished, too, until he rarely thought about it at all.

What makes this an especially useful and powerful tool is that you can practice it on yourself. It puts you in control, and you can measure your own progress over days and weeks. All you need to do is commit yourself to practicing the technique on a regular basis.

As we've seen, going to lunch at certain restaurants was a cue for Josh, so he needed to stay away from these places. Josh also needed to avoid the friend with whom he shared those lunches and the drugs afterwards. Certain friends can be cues. This can be hard to accept, but by doing so one avoids a lot of pain and difficult situations. If most of your friends are cues, it is extremely important for you to find a support system of people who are able to support you in staying away from destructive behaviors. Carefully evaluate the people around you and determine which of them are cues. Because even the mention of certain people's names may set up a feeling of wanting to return to old patterns, it is important to avoid thinking about their names or faces.

Some other things that can be cues include:

•Names of objects associated with compulsions. It is important to stay away from words that might trigger dangerous thoughts.

•Places. You know best which places you should avoid: in Josh's case, they were certain restaurants and bars where he met with his friend before doing drugs.

•Moods. Many people behave compulsively when they are feeling sad or depressed; they try to use the behavior as a pick-me-up. Even happy moods may be cues for those who have been using compulsive behavior as a reward for achievement.

•Paraphernalia. This is a big cue for just about everybody. For those recovering from drug addiction, it is important to get rid of bullets, scales, pipes, and needles, because these are all strong cues. For people quitting cigarette smoking, removing ashtrays, lighters and the smell of smoke in their environment is important.

This short list should help you get started on developing a cue list of your own. Start with the things that are mild cues and move on to the moderate and then severe ones. The biggest cues for just about everybody are thinking and talking about the old habit.

After making your list of cues—from mild to moderate to severe—the next step is to use your relaxation program and learn how to relax in response to all three kinds. Start with the mild cues and check your pulse. If you don't know how to check your pulse, have your doctor or a nurse show you how to do it. Put yourself in a relaxed situation so that your pulse gets very slow, and then think about one of the mild cues. If your pulse begins to increase, relax yourself and let your breathing slow down in order to reduce the pulse rate; then go back to thinking about the mild cue. In this way, you can work up to those cues that you have listed as severe or high-risk and relax consciously so that you won't be surprised by an exaggerated response when those cues come up in your everyday life.

This technique is called "desensitization," and it has proven very useful over the years to people who have phobias. (It is interesting to note that the phobic response, which is an anxiety response, is the same physiological response experienced in the urge to do drugs. That urge is often labeled as pleasurable by those who are addicted; the phobic or anxiety response is not pleasurable, but produces the same physiological sensations. It is only the label that is different, and we are the ones who label our feelings and responses.) The mind is a very powerful tool that we can use to change our responses (and relabel our feelings).

With time, Josh learned to relax and not respond with a drug urge to cues such as the restaurants where he used to lunch with his friend. He still has high pressure days much like those that set him up to use drugs in the first place, but now he uses relaxation techniques to respond to those pressures and to deal with his busy days. His overall ability to function effectively throughout the day has improved greatly.

As we have seen, recovering people need to be aware of behavioral cues and to stay away from high risk situations. Holiday parties and weddings are often situations to avoid during early recovery from addiction because they are often places where people use alcohol and other drugs. There is no point in putting yourself in situations where you have to constantly refuse things, so be good to yourself and avoid those situations. That means being honest with yourself and realizing that you don't have to prove your abstention by white-knuckling your way through parties. Instead, seek out events being held by supportive friends and family who will provide a healthy environment.

At the end of each day, recognize your improvements. Notice and give yourself credit for how much your urges and thoughts about compulsions have decreased each day. Take it one day at a time. Tell yourself that the destructive behavior is something you used to do. It is very important to think about your compulsive behaviors in the past tense.

Remember how powerful your thoughts are in setting up feeling states that can lead or not lead to a compulsive urge. Reinforce the knowledge that you are doing well and treating yourself well. Avoid any negative thoughts about yourself, as these may lead to destructive thinking and could lead to a relapse.

If you do relapse, please don't beat up on yourself, call yourself a failure, or give yourself a hard time. Many people who think poorly of themselves find that their hopelessness becomes their rationalization for using. So put the whip away and concentrate on getting back on your program of healing. Accept that you missed a cue, didn't avoid a situation you should have, or forgot to use the P.R.E. technique—and start again. You're worth it! Go back to your program of relaxation and positive reinforcement. Give yourself credit for the time you have avoided destructive behaviors and the progress you have made, and go back to taking care of yourself.

When the level of stress is greater, the support system must be greater as well. Here are some more practical tips to reduce the possibility of relapse:

•**Learn about your condition and how it has affected your life and the lives of your family members.** Books and pamphlets, workshops and counseling will help you learn more about the stages of healing and what to expect at different stages of recovery.

•**Learn to take good care of your body to promote a stable physical and mental attitude.** All of the things that you know about diet and exercise and their contribution to physical and mental stability are helpful to you now. It is dangerous to let yourself get on any kind of a roller coaster with diet, physical activity, or moods, because that can invite an urge to return to old behaviors. Watch out for foods that tend to trigger mood swings, like excessive amounts of sugar and caffeine.

•**Do not isolate yourself.** People become isolated as a result of addiction or compulsive behavior. Once sober or abstinent, it is important to develop healthy relationships with other people. It is too easy to close yourself off and set up an atmosphere of loneliness and self-pity, which in turn sets off an urge to indulge in destructive behaviors. So stay out and around people who are on a healing path.

•**Develop role models for healthy recovery.** Be on the lookout for recovering people to develop relationships with—people who are further along in recovery than you. They can provide guidance and help you assess what is normal at different stages of healing.

•**Become aware of secondary obsessions.** Early in the healing process, you may develop a kind of substitute addiction or obsession. In some cases it is a romantic obsession; in other cases it may be obsessive work or obsessive exercise. Alcoholics and addicts are particularly vulnerable to eating disorders and food addictions. Notice what a substitute behavior is doing for you and to you—what kind of need it may be meeting and what it may be keeping you from thinking or doing. It may be a behavior that you need for a while, like excessive work, to provide a structure so that you are not tempted to fall back into slippery places or old habits.

•**Enjoy the newness of life—the freshness and the innocence.** You may now notice pleasures that are simply a part of the joy of being alive. Enjoy this, taking pleasure in your natural surroundings and in the experience of living.

•**Understand assertiveness and its connection to abstinence and sobriety.** You may find yourself in situations in which it is very important to be able to say no. You may need to say things like "No, I don't want to," or "No, I don't want to go to that place anymore because it is a high risk for me." Assertiveness comes up as a big issue, and the ability to say no to situations that are not healthy and yes to situations that are is critical.

•**Manage your anxiety.** It is normal for you to be nervous and anxious at times. Still, you can learn relaxation skills and how to meditate to reduce stress without using drugs or alcohol.

Following are some suggestions to reduce the risk of using or returning to compulsive behavior in the first year of abstinence:

Limit conversations about the old lifestyle to four seconds. The four-second conversation technique is an important strategy. Conversations about drugs, for instance, can lead to thoughts about drugs, and these thoughts are potentially dangerous to your determination to get off and to stay off. The "four-second conversation" means you are literally allowed no more than four seconds to talk about the old lifestyle. Say something like, "I do not use drugs anymore, so please don't offer me any," or, "I don't want to discuss it." Any more than four seconds can be very dangerous. (You may add one more second if you used to deal or smuggle by adding "And I do not deal anymore, either.")

Stay sober as you abstain from drugs or compulsive behavior. I have seen very few people who could drink alcohol and stay away from their old habits. Because alcohol reduces inhibitions, people are more apt to fall into their old lifestyle when they drink.

Call your dealer (for former addicts and alcoholics). This is a very important strategy, but please do not undertake it alone. Have somebody with you who is not a drug user when you call your dealer so you won't get into trouble with this brief contact. Tell your dealer that you are not using anymore, and if you owe any money, pay it back.

Tell your family. One of the reasons we have families is to give and receive love and support, so please don't sell your family short. We need our families more than ever in times of stress.

Start a journal. This way you will be able to monitor your progress. It doesn't have to be anything fancy—just some notations on a daily basis about how you are feeling and how many days you have stayed away from your old lifestyle. It is something you can look back on later to give yourself credit for the progress you have made.

Change regular patterns. It helps to change some patterns you have in your life to break old habits. For instance, if you normally take a certain route home from work, and it goes past your favorite bar, find a different route. If you have a pattern of staying home and isolating yourself, find reasons to get out. These little changes can be a constant reminder and acknowledgment to yourself that you have some control over your life and the events that happen to you.

Change your environment. Sometimes people have to change their jobs if they have been engaging in destructive behavior at work. For safety reasons, sometimes they need to change where they live. Take a look at these factors and see if they apply to you.

Entertain at home. This is a helpful strategy, because when we entertain at home we have more control than we do when we go to someone else's house. We make the rules in our own homes and can be more comfortable saying things like, "Please don't come over when you're loaded, because I don't drink anymore."

Open up. Let those you care about know what's really going on with you. You will find that people who are really your friends and who really love you will appreciate this and feel closer to you.

Screen communications. It is important for you to break with all old lifestyle-related connections, so you may want to change your telephone number and/or install an answering machine. This allows you to screen your calls and gives you control.

Stop carrying cash. Cash in your pocket or purse often is a cue for drug purchase, compulsive spending, or other destructive behaviors that require money. Keep your available cash to about $25 or less. Have your paycheck deposited directly to the bank if necessary.

Get rid of credit cards and bank withdrawal cards. Never carry anything with you that will easily enable you to purchase something harmful to you. If you don't trust yourself, ask someone you do trust to help you with your finances while you find your balance.

Families

Taproot to the Past; Branch of Hope to the Future

The joy, freedom and struggles of healing are not only appreciated by the individuals who experience them, but also by other members of their families. In this context, the old expression, "hope springs eternal" speaks of the hope, across generations, that recovery brings. The recovery process that manifests itself in one person spreads backward to prior generations of parents, grandparents and great-grandparents, and forward to children, grandchildren, and great-grandchildren.

The first person in the family to choose a path of healing often feels very alone. At first, that aloneness can seem huge. The person who is the first to recover is a pioneer, and this is never an easy role. Many temptations are hard for this pioneer to avoid in early recovery. A person can do some things, however, to communicate his or her recovery to the family without alienating them:

Walk like you talk. The person who has it all together and lets others know this either in words or through attitudes is asking for trouble. This is because family members not in recovery tend to watch carefully. Words will usually be discounted. Actions and behavior that are consistent and loving, however, will impress people more. Family members will look for a consistency between words and behavior over time. They will want the newfound peace that they can see reflected in your eyes. They will hear the love in the sound of your voice rather than listen to specific words of advice. "Walk like you talk" refers to consistency that will impress the world over time.

Practice self-honesty. Focus your attention in the early stages of healing on yourself; this is called an "inventory" in twelve step programs. Because healing is a natural, predictable process, you will arrive at a point in your healing when you are ready to inventory or assess your life in an honest way. Part of this involves assessing your strengths and weaknesses and forgiving yourself for times when you've fallen short of your standards. It never involves taking someone else's inventory or making moral judgments on others—that is their job. Self honesty means taking your own inventory, working on forgiving yourself, and often making amends to others. (It is important to ask a supportive friend to help you make distinctions regarding situations when family members may need to be approached by you to clear up issues from the past.)

A good rule of thumb is to wait to approach family members until you are able to do so without blaming them. Approaching people openly without shaming or blaming them is a powerful tool for changing the nature of relationships. If you are in doubt, wait to approach a family member; spend more time in honest self-examination first.

Steer clear of judgments. Everyone has a wounded child deep inside them; this woundedness explains a lot of human behavior. In the area of parent/child relationships, it is important to remember that your parents are wounded, too. This doesn't mean you have to automatically forgive things that may have caused you harm. It simply means that once you can imagine your parent as a child who was wounded, the possibility that you will understand what motivated them will increase.

Parents who are emotionally wounded themselves can hardly provide adequate parenting for their children. Realizing this can help you to see your parent through the eyes of an adult rather than continuing to view them as if you were still a child.

The word "resentment" literally means to feel the same feeling over and over again, like a broken record. Looking at your parents from an adult perspective helps to break through that resentment.

It is often helpful to start thinking of your parents by their first names. You don't have to call them by that name out loud, but thinking the name reminds you that you are an adult and your parent is just another human being.

These techniques reduce the number and intensity of judgments. The more judgment is reduced, the greater the possibility for open and honest communication from adult to adult within your family.

Rethinking Family Roles

A number of authors have written books about the roles family members play in the healing process. In homes where the wounds run deep, a need for predictability often exists, which family roles fulfill. The anxiety produced by a chaotic household is reduced by clearly defined roles. The only problem is that these roles can and do become rigid—like prisons that people feel they cannot escape from. The "hero," the "mascot," the "clown," and the "scapegoat" are some of the roles played in these homes.

What has not been discussed, however, is the need for new roles.

When a family member chooses a path of healing, a vacuum is left that is felt by others in the family. They usually experience it as pain and emptiness.

With all this talk of roles, a play is a good analogy to explore family dynamics. If the roles are changed, then other aspects of the drama must change as well. As a friend of mine who is a playwright once suggested, when roles change we need to write ourselves a new play.

Because healing is a choice, people are automatically empowered by choosing it. Through this empowerment they have the ability to write their own scripts, and because so many people are new to this path, the sheer numbers of them can influence society as a whole. The potential for societal change is enormous.

I alluded to new societal roles at the very beginning of this book, where I discussed the pleasure of attending a peaceful rock concert. What a broadening concept it is to imagine an entire generation of children growing up in families that provide a spirit-enhancing, loving structure in which any daughter or son could flourish. All people who are actively working on their own healing are a participants in creating that kind of world.

In the meantime, however, profound emptiness sometimes is felt as a result of the redefinition of family roles. To continue the analogy of a play, consider the following scene:

It is Christmas Day. A family is gathering together, the only time during the year that the entire family gets together. The rest of the time the members are spread all around the country. The family name is Maloney and the family home, where the parents still live together, is in the suburbs of a major U.S. city.

Jim and Paula Maloney, the parents, are retired. Their three kids are now in their thirties. John and Maggie, the first and the middle child, respectively, each have two young children, and attend the Christmas gathering with their spouses. The youngest of the three Maloney children, Carla, is 31. She attends alone.

Carla is the first in the Maloney family to choose a healing path. Six months ago she stopped drinking alcohol and started reading books about being an adult child of an alcoholic. She also recently began to have memories about being molested by her uncle Greg when she was seven years old.

As Carla looks around the dining room table at dinner time, she sees her family through new eyes. She struggles with internal questions about her own upbringing and wonders whether she will have children herself someday. She also wonders if she will ever want to make that kind of commitment, given the possibility that she could pass on the alcoholism which is a part of her family's legacy.

She feels very much alone as she surveys her family. She is not a part of a couple, as everyone else is. She has no children, but everyone else does. Yet something still larger looms in her mind. She feels alone and empty because she doesn't fit in anymore.

It seems to Carla that there is a growing list of things that are not okay to talk about. She finds this new awareness unsettling, and makes a mental list for herself that she will write down later in her journal. Some of the things to avoid discussing are:

1. Her non-drinking status
2. Whether she will get married
3. Whether she will have children
4. The way her brother and sister discipline their children
5. Her Dad's drinking
6. Her memories of the sexual abuse
7. When she can get out of her current setting

Carla's tension level grows along with the list, and the list grows with her observations of her family over the following few days. She leaves the family holiday gathering feeling unsettled and empty. At times she feels that she may not return because it was so painful; she found herself wanting to join them in a drink just to block her feelings.

This could hardly be described as a merry Christmas. Carla is having a rough time of it, because it feels empty and alone to be the first and only person in a family to choose a new role. There are no guarantees that family members will be supportive. The suggestions I made earlier in this chapter to ease communication can help, but none is a panacea for the pain and loneliness.

If you anticipate going through something like this little play, by all means get support from others who have gone through something similar. Be kind to yourself by structuring family visits in such a way that you have the ability to leave for periods of time. Staying at a different home or at a motel during family visits may help you distance yourself from old patterns. Also try to arrange your own transportation so you will be mobile and can remove yourself at times to reduce stress.

Some of the painful roles that people in the early stages of healing take on *in the eyes of their families* are:

1. The Outsider The family may view the recovering person with suspicion. In some cultures, people who choose not to play their approved family role are shunned. This is accomplished by family members refusing to talk to the recovering person, or by talking on a surface level only, without really opening up.

2. The Betrayer When family members continue chemical dependency or abuse, the person who has chosen a path of healing may be forced to blow the whistle in order to stop it. As a result, anger may focus on the whistle-blower rather than the abuser.

3. The Scapegoat This occurs when family members try to reduce their own tension and shame level by blaming the recovering person for their problems. The family will attempt to keep the recovering person in whatever old family role that person formerly held. The universe abhors a vacuum, so this type of blaming occurs as a reflex reaction rather than as a conscious choice.

4. The Pioneer The first person to choose healing in a given family may take on a powerful, and at times lonely, role. The principles mentioned earlier in this chapter will help, but there are no simple guidelines.

Although your change influences those around you, you cannot control them or force them to choose a path of healing for themselves. This is easier to accept when you remember that no one could have forced you to choose a healing path either.

Sometimes you will need periods when you have little contact with family, so that you can gain perspective and continue your own healing. For some people, part of healing is to develop a new extended family to meet family needs in a healthier way. Extended family and friends who are freely chosen are an important part of the healing process.

Even the considerable pain of emptiness is preferable to being a part of a family group in which active abuse or addiction are present. Emptiness and loneliness, like other feelings, do not last forever. Sometimes the best thing to do with loneliness is simply to acknowledge it.

There are no rigid roles in a recovering family. Instead, individuals are aware of needs and wants, and communicate those to family members. This requires skill in negotiation and communication, which must be learned in order to maintain a flourishing, flexible, spirit-enhancing, interdependent family system.

The following is a story of family recovery and healing that spans several generations. It is told by one of the family members, the mother of three children. She and her courageous family are a continuing source of inspiration to me.

> The recovery of my family, as opposed to my personal recovery, is difficult to isolate. The two are intertwined and offer lots of food for thought.
>
> I remember being at a convention for codependency. One of the workshops asked participants to set up a family. The people posed in whatever postures they would have within this family. The exercise allowed me to see very clearly how each person's role in a family affects those of others, as well as the family as a whole—the roles are like building blocks. So the recovery of even one person changes the whole family.
>
> Six years into my personal recovery, I know my family is very different than it was six years ago. In our family, my "middle" child started it. She was the pioneer in recovery and healing. Looking back, I am amazed at the level of denial I experienced about the drugs, alcohol and woundedness. I knew I drank too much, and that I binged and purged. I knew my middle daughter was doing some cocaine. I knew that my son and my son-in-law both smoked pot. Yet I was only mildly concerned.
>
> Then my daughter got help and quit cocaine. I watched her do that and I knew I wasn't any different than she was—I just used alcohol instead of cocaine. Her change of position changed my position.
>
> I have since become aware of my old roles in my families—both my birth family and that of my husband and my children. In the second case, I subtly projected an image of dependence and neediness to which my children responded. My oldest

child, a son, was thrown into the position of father at seventeen when my husband and I divorced. He was very responsible then and helped out financially so we could make ends meet. What a shock it was to realize years later that my children viewed me as weak and fragile.

We are now all in very different relationships with each other. My daughters and I are good friends, but we lead quite separate lives. I used to believe that once my children were grown and out of the house they should be independent of me; that meant I had done a good job of parenting. Now I believe that children still need parenting as adults, and that I can help my children both financially and emotionally in a healthy, supportive way without fostering unhealthy dependency. When my middle child was leaving her husband, she and I rented a house and lived there with her two children for a year and a half. It was a great experience for all of us; we learned from each other. And I think she and I came out of the experience less dependent, yet truly closer than we were going in.

I feel a strong bond with my youngest daughter, and I have enormous admiration for her recovery, which resulted from her watching and listening to my middle child and myself. I have watched her grow and change, taking care of herself and her needs. All of that has done a lot for her family. Although her husband has not chosen recovery yet, I see that he has benefited from her work, as have her children.

Today, the girls are very close friends and support each other in their recovery, each doing it in their own style.

While my daughters and I have been working on a healing path over these last few years, my son has remained living in the same house where we all lived together—symbolic, I think, of the lack of growth in his life. Metaphorically, I see him still holding the same position in that family portrait we started with, but the rest of us are gone. How painful that must be for him. We have chosen to ignore him, because he ignores us. I am in the process right now of changing that. I have talked with him on the telephone recently, and I was allowed to see that he really does care about us. He ignores us because to do otherwise is too painful for him. I want to change my way of dealing with him and stop ignoring him. So for now, I have decided to call him up periodically and let him know I care about him.

I was able to rid myself of my anger with my mother before she died. I have an aunt, a sister of my mother, who lives in the east. She told me how different I was when she came out to see us (after I chose recovery), that I was so much more approachable and human. I remember when she had come out while I was still drinking, and how inconvenient it was having her around. The real reason was that her visit interfered with my drinking and smoking. She came out this year for my daughter's wedding and played the role my mother would have if she were still alive. That would have not been possible without our recovery.

I'm in a relationship now with a wonderful man. I'm vulnerable and see parts of myself that I wouldn't have if I had stayed alone. But it is worth the work to have so much fulfillment and joy in my life. I get a lot of good, healthy support from my women's group, my AA sponsor, and my daughters.

I used to spend a lot of time with my stepmother and her daughter. They are a part of my family, but now, because I know that much of those relationships were really based on alcohol and cigarettes, I don't see them, but we do stay in touch. So many of my relationships with people were based not on who we were, but if and what we drank and smoked, and how much!

All this change and growth in the family has to have a positive effect on my grandchildren. I know there is still plenty of dysfunction, and there will always be work to do. But we are healthier and happier than ever before, and that has to have a bearing on the lives of my grandchildren and those to come.

Deep Culture and its Effect on the Family

A natural part of the healing process is to ask, "Who am I—what are my beliefs and values?" To reach toward the branch of hope that is the future, people must first reach down deep, to the taproot of the past.

In the rush to assimilate into a new country and to acquire a sense of belonging immigrant groups often give up their sense of cultural identity. In this and other ways, the process of assimilation for first-generation immigrant families is similar regardless of their ethnocultural backgrounds.

Each new group that comes to America faces some prejudice and struggle. Vietnamese-Americans, for example, are experiencing struggles similar to those of the Russian and Irish immigrants at the turn of the century. (One thing the Irish had that made their situation easier, however, was a facility with the English language.)

Too often, cultural groups throw the baby out with the bathwater, so to speak. Shame of poverty is a powerful force, causing families to choose not to speak of the past. Immigrants may avoid family history if it is connected with poverty, hopelessness and oppression. Also, some people confuse the political and economic climate that forced them to emigrate with their culture as a whole. This can leave considerable confusion of identity in the next generation.

Shame and identity confusion can occur across any ethnocultural line. European-Americans experience shame, too. Until recently, people who emigrated from European countries did not even have a designation. Even now they are often lumped together, discounted as whites or Caucasians when, in fact, each European-American family has a distinct heritage, just as other ethnocultural family groups do. Irish Americans, for instance, have a very different heritage than Russian-Americans, who in turn have a very different heritage than Italian-Americans.

Because of my own familiarity with the group, and because over forty-seven million people in this country can trace some Irish heritage, I will use Irish-Americans as an example of a cultural group with a distinct background and heritage.

During the mid-eighteen hundreds, when the potato famine spread across Ireland, the population dwindled from ten million in 1840 to six and a half million in 1850. Many children were orphaned. Because someone had to raise these children, the Catholic Church stepped in. (It was not the business of the church to raise children, but there was no one else to do it.) The Irish family, which had traditionally been a strong unit, was broken.

Discipline, authority, rigid structure, and suffering-as-virtue replaced traditional values and served the purposes of both controlling and providing a structure for the upbringing of thousands of abandoned youngsters. But these qualities were no substitute for love and the sense of belonging provided by a family. As a result, many youngsters were raised without family structure, and did not know how to be parents to their own children.

Many of these children eventually emigrated to the U.S., Canada, or other countries in hopes of a better life. They fled from starvation and from political, economic and religious oppression. In their flight they carried a deep shame of poverty, as well as a confusion between poverty and Irishness—they saw the two things as one and the same. Pride in being Irish and all that it meant was often lost in this confusion. As a result, secrecy and shame took its place.

Because of these circumstances, many Irish Americans today know little or nothing of their Irish culture. This has a profound effect on family, bonding, and the self-esteem of children growing up devoid of a rich heritage.

Studies have shown that a part of self-esteem is related to a developing sense of self as a member of an ethnic group. Many families, however, raise children who have no idea of their rich cultural heritage. Learning about this heritage raises self esteem because it answers important questions such as "Who am I?" and "What are my culture's enduring values?"

In the healing process, people need to spend time learning about their ethnocultural heritage and making distinctions and choices about what they wish to keep of their heritage and what they choose to reject. It is a personal journey that starts during Stage II healing and extends to Stage IV. At that time, the cultural values that people choose to keep become integrated as part of their sense of self.

Without a sense of deep cultural heritage a person may be rootless, because there may be no sense of self to draw from during times of stress. People who have a deep cultural taproot usually have some well-thought-out answers to the questions "Who am I?" and "Where do I belong?" Something is gained at a deep level that can be offered to succeeding generations.

Conducting Family Research

If you know very little about your family cultural background, treat this as a mystery story. Collect clues and piece them together. Begin by interviewing relatives for information and stories about your family. This is a sifting and sorting process through which you will make choices that will affect not only you as an individual, but also your children and their children as well. The sense of self that is enhanced as a result of knowing your heritage will enhance your whole family.

Here is the story of a man who has struggled with the issue of what to keep of the old heritage and what to leave behind.

> My name is Walter. I am a first-generation Chinese-American. Born and raised in Hong Kong, I first came to this country at the age of seventeen to receive my college education. It was a decision made by my parents, and I can remember having little or no say about it.
>
> Both of my parents' educations were interrupted when Japan attacked and occupied China during the Second World War. Their regret led them to believe that none of their children should have the same misfortune. In fact, studying was stressed as the number one priority in my childhood.
>
> At the age of six, I was sent to a Catholic school that was famous for academic achievement. The school was run by a group of Spanish priests. It was there that I first learned how to speak English, the official language in Hong Kong. I proceeded to spend the next eleven years at the same school.
>
> The academic workload was always very heavy. There was endless homework and test preparation every day. There were

also numerous incidents of physical, emotional and spiritual abuse. The school demanded absolute obedience, and violation of rules often resulted in physical punishment, such as spanking or public humiliation in front of the whole school during the morning assembly. I, like most of the other students, experienced a sizable share of abuse. Yet despite all of these experiences, most of the parents, including mine, were openly proud that their children were able to attend such a highly regarded school.

After I survived the initial year in first grade and finished first, I was rewarded with permission to skip the second grade and join the third grade directly. This brought about more abuse, mostly from my peers. The experience of being labeled as the "genius" and left in the same classroom all day with a group of physically bigger and taller classmates is one that I will never forget.

Most of my childhood was spent in study; I had very little time just to play. And in the spare time I did have, I was strongly encouraged to play with games and toys that were designed to sharpen and train my mind.

Life at home was no different than school life—my parents also demanded absolute obedience. A lot of the time I had to anticipate and guess what was in my parents' minds and react ahead of time. Simply put, a smart kid will always know what to say or do without an adult giving him explicit directions. Time and time again I received material and/or verbal rewards for being able to follow this rule. Time and time again I was shamed with messages like "you should have known better" for not being able to guess right. It's no wonder I have so much trouble now, as an adult, asking for assistance even when I know I need it.

Both of my parents are adult children of addicts and alcoholics. They grew up with little guidance, and both assumed the role of a lost child in their respective families. My grandfather was an opium addict, spending most of his life in his bedroom on his "opium bed." This is a rosewood bed without any mattress, about twice the size of a king-size bed, specially designed to allow a couple of people to lie down comfortably while they are smoking opium.

My father was considered by many to be a devoted family man because he spent all of his time outside work with the family. I remembered feeling strange because he did not have any friends; I was not encouraged to have any friends of my own. The message I got, though not verbally communicated to me, was that as long as the family stays close together, no friends are needed. My father was commended by my relatives for sacrificing himself for the sake of his family. To them and to him, this is love.

My father is also a very angry man. He has a tremendous amount of rage buried inside him. Once ignited, he can be very intimidating. I was often reminded by my mother to avoid making him mad. I considered this to be one of the most important survival lessons for me as I grew up, and it made me emotionally detached. Even today, after four years of therapy and recovery, a lot of fear and sadness toward my father still remains in me. I attribute the feeling of sadness to my recovery, because whenever I am with my father I can now feel a strong desire to get close to him, but his emotional wall is still there and probably always will be. Still, by understanding that he may never change, I am able to establish a better relationship with him.

Like my father, my mother is also an abandoned child. She was brought up by an aunt after her mother remarried. In those days, it was looked upon as a wise decision, because in all probability my mother would have been discriminated against by her stepfather and his family.

My mother always considered herself a simple woman and easily satisfied. In a sense, she is right. She expects her husband and her children to consider her the most important person in their lives. Straight and simple! She told me repeatedly that "If you love your mother, then think of me first on everything." To her, this is respect, and respect is such a big word in Chinese families.

In the old days, if a father asked his son to kill himself and he did not oblige, then the son was not showing any respect. Such thinking still exists to a certain degree in a lot of families today. Parents tell their children that everything they have done has been for their children. In return, they expect unquestioning respect! A famous Chinese saying goes, "There is no fault or mistake in parents," and my mother used to say this a lot. The message in this is that you can wait for your turn to demand respect and obedience when you become a parent. This is a dysfunction that has been passed along in our culture for generations.

My parents did not get along well. However, they seldom got into arguments. Part of the reason was that whenever my father got angry, my mother would just be quiet. This proved to be a very effective way to calm my father down, but her emotions did not go away. She just "stuffed" it (her own words). At the same time, my dad did not dispose of his anger appropriately, either. He was stuffing most of his anger, too. This kind of emotion-stuffing would go on for a long time. Then I would step in as the peacemaker to "save their marriage," a role that I began to assume when I was three years old, and continued to perform until my parents finally separated after thirty-three years of marriage. (That was two years before I began my road to recovery.) After all, as another Chinese saying goes, "It is the duty of a son to see that his parents are together and get along fine."

Today, I am still receiving pressure from my relatives to perform this "duty" from time to time. My boundary of accepting this part of my culture is constantly being challenged; I have been criticized and described as "Americanized" and as "betraying my culture." This is a price that I have to pay, and I do so gladly. The benefits of healing far outweigh the guilt that comes with not doing things the old way.

Many of the family issues identified in the preceding story are universal and cross all ethnocultural lines. Still, the deep sense of identity gained by knowing where you come from enhances the healing process.

Take the time to explore the mystery of family. It will pay dividends in enhanced self esteem, and boost your own healing.

When interviewing family members, try to be as nonjudgmental as possible. Remember that their histories are very different from yours. Ask open-ended questions and observe what directions they take in answering the questions; let them take the lead.

Many of your older relatives will have survived some very rough times. Memories can bring up pain, so be patient and remember that whatever information a relative presents is like gold. Sift and sort what is useful for you to know, remembering that the information is presented from their own interpretation of events. Just listen openly, take what you can use, and leave the rest.

Dreams

Blueprints of the Recovery Process

Dreams are critical milestones in healing, for they reflect the connection between the body and the soul. As such, dreams are the landscape on which the internal drama of growth and conflict are expressed. Many types of dreams occur at different stages in the healing process, and recovering people usually experience fascinating dreams. When chemicals are removed from the body, dream recall improves. People have active rapid eye movement cycles and remember their dreams with fascination. Here are the kinds of dreams common to those who have chosen the path of healing:

Nightmares

The following example is one that has many variations, but the message from the self is loud and clear.

> I keep having the same dream. I am being strangled by a faceless person. I struggle and struggle, and before they strangle me or I get away, the dream ends. I wake up frightened in the middle of the night. I want this dream to stop.

There are many versions of this dream. In most of them the person's life is threatened, usually by an unknown attacker.

This dream is, of course, a nightmare. Such a dream occurs when the self is screaming for attention. When people continue to ignore their needs, a nightmare will often occur that is the psyche's equivalent of hitting you with a two-by-four. The dreams usually become more and more dramatic until the dreamer pays attention.

Such a nightmare that is repetitive in nature is a signal that something important in the psyche is demanding attention. The man who had the nightmare related above was unaware for a very long time that he was cut off from his own spirituality. The dream started when he was eleven years old and recurred periodically in his life. After a period of time when he had begun to take care of his own emotional and spiritual needs, the nightmare stopped. (It is interesting to note that in his nightmare, he continued to be eleven years old, even as he grew to adulthood. As he let himself slow down, reduced his workload and played more, the nightmares stopped. His inner child was asking for healing and acknowledgment and finally received it.

Another type of nightmare pattern involves a chase. A person is being pursued, sometimes by a faceless person, sometimes by a known pursuer. This nightmare can be very frightening; the dreamer may wake up in a full fight-or-flight adrenaline reaction.

There are several causes of this type of nightmare. One factor can be physical instability. In the first stage of healing, people frequently have some combination of physical problems, particularly those who were addicted to stimulant drugs.

In the chapter on Stage I healing I discuss the importance of proper diet and exercise in early recovery. If this is attended to, these types of nightmares decrease. On the other hand, stimulants like caffeine can aggravate nightmares like this because the body reacts with an adrenaline rush, even during sleep.

Another type of nightmare is called the "using" dream. It is a kind of dream that people in early chemical dependency recovery (Stage I) experience. In the dream, alcohol or drugs are offered to the dreamer. Sometimes the dreamer takes the chemical; sometimes not. In any event this dream is usually an indication that the psyche is trying to catch up with the person's decision to stay clean and sober. It does not necessarily mean that the person will use or relapse in waking life.

Nightmares are often caused by fear of the unknown. When people are chased in dream reality, it is different than being chased in waking reality. You, as the dreamer, can stop, turn around, and ask, "Why are you chasing me?" Often the pursuer turns out to have a gift or some information to give the dreamer. When the fear is faced and the dreamer stops running, the whole dream changes. By stopping, people empower themselves. Before you go to sleep, resolve to face the fear—you are likely to gain some important information about yourself that you will never learn by running.

Sometimes the pursuer is a shadowy, dark figure. This can be a part of yourself that is trying to get attention and acknowledgment. Improvement and change will occur by turning and facing the fear. We all have a dark side and can benefit by learning more about it.

There is a technique called "lucid dreaming" through which you can relax yourself before going to sleep, remember your dream, and ask yourself what you want to understand about the dream. With practice you can learn to re-enter a dream to gather more information. This is an empowering experience.

In the healing process, people learn that a part of them in their waking life stands back and observes in any situation. Through lucid dreaming you learn to develop that same healthy observer role in your dreams. This way the observer part of you can fulfill a role as witness and protector, both in waking and in dreaming states.

Relapse Prevention Dreams

Because dreams are often metaphors, it is important to suspend the waking ego and see the metaphorical level of a dream. If you can do this, you can possibly recognize a type of dream that can act as an early warning system to prevent relapse. One example comes from a dreamer who is a diver in his waking life. He dreamed he was going on a dive at the Cayman Islands (which was about to happen in his waking life). The dive was a cave exploration, but he forgot to take a buddy with him and to attach his oxygen tanks. He woke up feeling scared, but also knowing that the dream was important.

This dreamer was recovering from sex and love compulsions, and was close to a recovery anniversary at the time of the dream. As mentioned earlier, anniversaries are always vulnerable points for relapse. This dream was an early warning signal of danger.

He was asked as part of a dream group to reenter the dream in a state of meditation, to see if the outcome would change. He did, and brought the dream group with him as diving buddies. This time he checked to make sure he had his regulator and oxygen with him. Toward the end of the dream he realized that he had been diving only three feet under the surface of the water! He had not taken his oxygen tanks earlier because they had not been necessary. When he emerged from the meditation, he realized what a gift this dream was for his recovery. His level of awareness was raised ahead of time, and thus he avoided relapse. He learned that he could trust himself to prepare for the level of risk he was about to face.

By keeping a dream journal it is possible to maintain an increased level of awareness regarding danger. People should then increase their support at vulnerable times in their lives.

Memory Recall Dreams

In a number of dreams experiences from the past are presented to us in various ways. This is the psyche's attempt to make some sense of an experience. One type of recall dream involves traumatic memory. Sometimes experiences that were traumatic are forgotten by the conscious mind, but the body and soul remember and store the information just as a computer stores away data.

A person may experience memory recall as a regular dream, or, at a more intense level, as a nightmare when the psyche is asking for healing. Portions of events from the past may be replayed as a dream or as dream fragments. Sometimes real events that are too disturbing for the conscious mind are replayed as bits and snatches of scenes. In such a case, lucid dreaming can be used to help recall a memory.

When the memory being recalled is upsetting or traumatic, some help in the form of therapy is a good idea. Remembering traumatic events is stressful, and as I mentioned earlier, it is important to increase your support when you are experiencing more stress.

Memory recall dreams often appear in Stage III healing, when events from childhood that have been repressed are also surfacing in waking life. Often the dream will present information in a veiled manner so that the person has time to work it out. Remember that the psyche won't present too much to handle at any point in time; be gentle with yourself. Do not try to force the situation. Bits and pieces will be presented as you are able to handle the information.

Traumatic memories are not the only kind that present themselves. Both neutral material and pleasant material can be recalled as well. When you feel that a dream is still with you after waking, chances are something more needs to be explored about the dream.

Here are two examples of recall dreams, the first from a man and the second from a woman:

> Wednesday Night, June 13
> Scene: Childhood home, Trinidad, Colorado
> Am home alone with Dad at the old house. We are watching TV together. I am thirteen or fourteen years old. I am
> wearing the pajamas I was wearing the night Dad was beaten.
> Dad gets up and walks out of the front door.
> The wind picks up and begins to blow very strongly.
> The wind blows all the doors open.
> All the lights are on in the house.
> I get up from the floor where I have been sitting and go down the hallway to my sister's room. There is a computer there.
> She is sitting at the computer. The screen is blank.
> I decide to go to bed.

I notice the wind is really howling. I go to the front room. Windows are open. The door is open, wind is blowing through the house. The curtain is blowing in the wind.
I close the front door and go to the kitchen.
The kitchen windows are open. I am afraid burglars will come into the house.
The kitchen curtain is blowing into the house.
I turn on the lights outside the house because I am afraid of burglars.
The curtain tears in two. I try to grab it. It comes off the window with the curtain rod.
The curtain rod is twisted.
I put it down. I think my mom will fix it when she gets home.
I notice that there is a television on a counter where the refrigerator used to be.
I am afraid that burglars will break in.
The television is blank with snow. The channel dials show my ages instead of channel numbers.

The dreamer was remembering an incident when two men in ski masks came into his house and held him at gunpoint while they beat his father. In the dream there is poor protection—open doors and windows where the wind from the outside can enter and blow through. A lack of protection, safety, boundaries is strongly felt.

In his waking life, the dreamer's mother has died years after the incident. Her absence in the dream meant that the dreamer would not be able to help to put his world right again.

Nothing was 'adding up' in this person's life as a result of this incident. His world was turned upside down, and he felt he could no longer count on anything. A kitchen "counter" and a computer are metaphors for this in the dream.

When asked to reenter the dream in an active way, the dreamer understood that the TV sets were there so that he could retrieve memories safely by changing channels; the numbers on the dial represented ages at which memories occurred. Through active imagination he was able to understand the dream and retrieve memory without being overwhelmed by the experience.

Here is the second recall dream:

> I dreamed that people who had committed crimes or offenses of some nature had had their arms cut off as punishment, but only from the elbows down. My role in the dream was to assist these people with no arms to live normal lives. I wanted to help them learn to use their shorter arms in daily life.

The dreamer was a woman who was recovering from sexual abuse by her father. In the dream she has disarmed him for her own safety. (She chose the arms because they were used to hold her when he rubbed against her body.) The dream indicates not only visual, but emotional recall, because she felt scared and "icky" in the dream. It also illustrates the fact that a tremendous amount of healing has taken place, because she is beginning to forgive the perpetrator, as shown by the work she does to help the people with short arms in the dream.

Protecting oneself is the first level of self-care in a lucid dream of an attack or violation. Going beyond that to develop a life as a survivor is a task undertaken after much healing has occurred, as was the case with this dreamer.

Symbols

This is not intended as a primer on dream interpretation, but rather a prompting for you to begin to honor the dream for its power and wisdom as a healing tool. Because all people every person have their own history, they must be their own dream interpreter. Symbols are very specific to individuals. For example, a woman in early healing as an adult child of an alcoholic presented the following dream:

> I was manufacturing jeans, and I went to look at a manufacturing plant in Russia. I wanted to produce the jeans there using American capitalism as an economic base.

The dreamer wanted to understand her dream. She said she felt "peaceful" after waking. When asked about what jeans meant to her, she said they were casual, free, and comfortable clothing.

This was a breakthrough dream for her healing. She was a person who wanted to be freer, less constricted and more creative in her life. With this dream she was allowing more freedom inside herself as she brought something free and new to infuse the Russian economy with life. Not long after the dream she began writing for pleasure for the first time in her life. This was something she had always wanted to do.

In addition, the dream may have had another level of meaning. Sometimes puns are presented in a dream; in this one, "jeans" turned out to be a pun for "genes" This woman learned she was pregnant soon after the dream—she was undergoing artificial insemination around the time she experienced it.

Many dreams have several levels of meaning. The levels do not all need to be logical in a linear way; some levels can even seem to our logical minds to be in conflict with one another. Anything is possible in dream reality, and because of this it is important to suspend the ego and the logical, linear mental process when examining a dream. Instead, follow your heart and your gut response to the dream.

People often are presented in dreams with symbols they do not understand with their conscious mind. The symbol is often understood when we least expect it. I once had a dream where a huge mushroom grew in front of a thatched, Irish country cottage. After meditating on the symbol, it became clear to me that the mushroom provided two things that I needed and valued. First, it provided shelter for the occupant of the house (me), and second, it gave me a sense of renewal, as mushrooms grow out of decay. The mushroom was a powerful symbol, much to my surprise—a testimony to beauty and creativity arising from rubble or refuse. There are four things you can do when presented with a symbol you don't understand:

1. Meditate on it

2. Reenter the dream to gather more information

3. Notice if the dream symbols are presented in your waking life in some form

4. Research the symbol; read about it and try to gain a more complete understanding of it.

Dreams in Which Children Appear

In dreams, sometimes children are exactly that—children. Sometimes, however, they are symbolic. The following example is from a female dreamer:

> I was sitting at a table in an outdoor restaurant by the sea. A man came by with a baby. I realized he was my ex-husband. The baby was six months old, and he handed me the baby, kissed me on the cheek, and walked off. I looked at the baby, who was not smiling. The baby was wearing a fine metal sheath over her head, like knights used to wear, only the sheath was made of very light mesh and covered her skull.

This dreamer had been through a divorce six months before, and the baby represented the dreamer's spiritual and emotional condition. She reported that although the baby didn't smile initially, she smiled in a later dream.

On one level, the baby was the dreamer's inner child, and on another she was the dreamer's progress since the divorce. The dreamer had experienced a resurgence of her own creative expression in the six months after the divorce, shown by the fact that the baby was healthy and well nourished. The sheath on the baby's head provided protection, which was important because the infant had been in the custody of the ex-husband. The dreamer was reclaiming her inner child, and the dream spoke of emotional and spiritual renewal for the dreamer and progress in her new life.

Spiritual Dreams

All dreams are spiritual in nature, because they connect the body and soul. Some dreams are special because they signify special rites of passage from one stage of development to the next.

1. Initiation Dreams These come in many forms, but usually a pattern exists. Often they occur during the transition from Stage II to Stage III healing. Here is a typical example:

> I get into a boat. It is open and a man is rowing. The boat drifts down the river and we come to an island. The man nods in my direction to leave the boat. I do and am greeted by a group of smiling women of all ages. They give me flowers and take me to a special place where they surround me, and a special ritual is celebrated.

Here is another example of a spiritual initiation dream from a woman who is an incest survivor:

> I got on an open-air paddleboat to go for a ride. It was somewhere in the South. The air was moist and warm, the landscape swampy. As the ride got underway, I began to notice that only women were on board, my therapist among them. The voices of the women slowly formed a rhythmic chant, growing louder and stronger. I suddenly realized I was at the center of their circle. As we docked and I was led up the gangway, I could feel their voices running through me, the rhythm pulsing in my veins. A door opened to a room with a panel of revered women seated at a table. The woman in the center of the table was dressed as a high priestess. I knew immediately that she was very important.

> Upon the opening of the door into the room I realized the air was filled with the essence of my grandfather. To breathe in that air was to take in his essence—to feel him, all that he was, all that he did to me. I held my breath as I was led before the priestess, and above the chanting I could hear her shouting "breathe it in, breathe it in, it's the only way." I fought with myself, not wanting to feel my abuser, yet needing air. Their chants and shouts to breathe filled the room, and with a scream I finally breathed in and awoke.

When asked how she felt upon awakening the dreamer answered, "serene." Women often have a variation of this dream as a rite of passage. It is a recognition and acknowledgment of spiritual healing that has been undertaken and accomplished. The group of women in the dream witness the dreamer's rite of passage and celebrate her new life. Often a wise-woman or wise-man is presented in the dream. This person serves as a kind of guide.

People who experience this type of dream have come very far on their spiritual and emotional healing journey. Self-love is one of the hallmarks of a dream in which a dreamer is lovingly surrounded by members of her or his own sex.

2. Death and Rebirth Dreams The healing journey is often compared to a death and rebirth process. Most cultures have myths concerning salvation, which is usually offered after a symbolic death/rebirth process. At the junction from Stage III to Stage IV (usually about three to five years into healing) people often have this type of dream. Here is a typical example:

> I am crouched down low in the forest. A group of small birds are pecking at my body. I rise up and as I do I turn into an eagle and soar away.

For this dreamer, this was a powerful "phoenix" experience. The dreamer rose out of his dark night of the soul just as people in recovery often do by making a new life for themselves. The new life is based on faith and spiritual principles, fueled by a higher power with a spiritual foundation.

Flying dreams are often spiritual in nature. The soul, removed from the shackles of hopelessness, can now soar.

Dreams of Family Healing and Recovery

Because recovery affects the whole family, other members in addition to the identified recovering person are undergoing extensive healing at the same time. Partners of alcoholics, for example, undertake an internal journey that parallels the new roles they experience in their relationships.

An example of this is the dream of a woman who was three months into the divorce process. She was setting up a new life for herself and her children after a fifteen-year marriage had ended. Her ex-husband was still in denial of his alcoholism at the time of the dream she described:

> A house—very big. My parents seem to be part owners. Also the Elmers (a Catholic family in the neighborhood I grew up in, who had ten children and lived in a tiny, filthy, unkempt house). Pinky and Jay (Elmer) will get the large bedroom with the fireplace. (Jay was a raging alcoholic.) I find a pair of Pinky's earrings: one is a fireplace, the other a diamond or something, but I lose them. I seem to be cleaning the rooms. Francine (my older son's kindergarten teacher) is there. I find a floppy disk I've loaned to Tom Elmer—it's a disk from my WordPerfect set, and something has been spilled on it, the disk is covered with something sticky. I am furious because now it's ruined. People seem to be preparing for a permanent arrangement of bedrooms. I wonder where the ten kids will sleep.

The dreamer was undergoing a personal metamorphosis, both in her dream and her waking world. In both she was moving, rearranging her life. The house represented her self was peopled by an alcoholic family she knew from her childhood. She never wanted to become like them, but she ended up marrying an alcoholic anyway. She was coming to terms with this and wondering at the end of her dream how the alcoholism would affect her children.

Recovery has a profound effect on the next generation. And although life isn't perfect (WordPerfect was a pun), it is much improved from the "filthy, unkempt" house of the past. In this new house people seem to have a choice as to how things will be arranged. The dreamer had an active role in cleaning the rooms, just as she was coming to terms with and cleaning up her past to make way for the future.

Family Legacy Dreams

Just as family healing occurs in dreams, intergenerational healing and wisdom may be passed along as well. Even when people are wounded at the soul level, they are sometimes able to communicate in a dream in a way that goes beyond the ego and the woundedness. Their higher self and a family member's higher self can sometimes communicate as a result. Here is a personal example from a series of dreams that revealed information about my own family:

> I am sitting in my father's living room. He is presenting a small, pewter deer to me as a gift and saying "I want you to have this."

I realized immediately that this was an important dream. The deer was a very specific family symbol—I am from an old Irish family where the stag is a symbol on the family coat of arms.

This was a legacy dream because my father, who presents the deer, was close to dying at the time. I knew that my father was passing on the family legacy, and because the symbol was a deer (doe) rather than a male stag, I felt that my father was especially handing down the female family legacy.

After I experienced the dream, I decided to tell my father about it. Sharing the dream gave me a new closeness and openness with my father, who opened up about his deceased wife (my mother) and talked about their marriage. This was very healing to me; I had wanted more information about her mother. The doe was also a pun in this dream about family legacy. The second meaning of the word "doe" refers to financial inheritance, which I did not ever consider to be a factor before the dream.

Legacy dreams come in many forms, but it is not unusual for antiques or old jewelry to be presented by a family member in a dream. This commonly represents some important and healing information about the family. When a dream is intergenerational, there is often a sense of importance attached to it. The dream stays with the dreamer and is remembered with great clarity. These are special dreams and often represent turning points in a person's life.

There are also many surprises in family legacy dreams. Even in families where there are many wounds, there are also gifts that are handed down from one generation to another.

To dream is to hope. Hope is defined as knowing that what we desire is also possible. When we recall dreams, we foster hope, and when we foster hope we build spiritual muscle and we soar. Honor yourself in your healing process by paying attention to your dream life. Our own dreams are among our greatest teachers and healers.

The Body

Storehouse of Information

Although the body contains a wealth of information, people often have mixed feelings toward their own bodies. This is particularly true of people who were abused as children; abused children learn to shut off physical sensations and thus carry a sense of being out of touch with their own bodies well into recovery. This must be unlearned, because true healing involves body, spirit, mind and emotions.

Even for people who learn to shut off physical needs and responses, however, the body continues to send messages. There are constant reminders of this. Chronic weariness, medical symptoms of illness and physical limitations are signals being sent by a body that has been pushed too far too long without receiving the care it needs.

The internal organs often receive the most severe beating, especially for those in early recovery from chemical dependency. This is why I cannot overemphasize the importance of education about proper nutrition as part of a healing program.

For people who grow up in a stressful environment, the body is constantly under stress. The internal organs feel this stress, especially when repeated adrenaline reactions occur. I mentioned the effect of stress on the nervous system earlier; other organs, especially the pancreas, liver, and kidneys, react to stress as well. Just as you may feel tired and in need of rest after a period of stress, a person's internal organs also need rest after experiencing the stress of growing up in a tense, frightening environment. They also need rest after chemicals have been removed.

It takes time for the organs to heal. Take the pancreas, for instance. It has the job of regulating the body's blood sugar level, and in early recovery, it needs to stabilize. Coffee, sugar, and cigarettes all increase stress on the pancreas, slowing down its healing process. By being gentle and reducing or eliminating these substances, you let the pancreas do its job and heal.

Some people spend a lifetime learning to be tough and tolerating discomfort and pain. To heal, they need to reverse this process and be more aware of bodily sensations. They need to honor the body by responding with appropriate care when the body sends a message.

In Stage I recovery, people begin to notice their bodies and to respond. By Stage III, they realize that there is a connection between how their body is feeling and their emotions. Here is an example of that link in the form of a story about a woman with whom I once worked. She was leaving Stage II and entering Stage III, with its heightened awareness.

After a year and a half of sobriety, Cheryl had become involved in a relationship with a man. When they had been dating for about six months, he invited her to go house hunting with him one weekend. He said that he needed a house for himself, and he wanted her input as to what house might be a good choice for him. In the process of house hunting, however, he began to make it very clear that he really wanted to move into a house with her. This was a surprise to Cheryl, because they had never discussed such a thing and had only been dating for six months.

Clearly, Cheryl did not feel ready to consider moving in with this man—she was taken aback by his suggestion that they move in together. But Cheryl was at a point in her healing where she was just beginning to become aware of feelings. As an adult child of an alcoholic, she had learned to shut down her feelings and become numb.

Here is the process that she went through to become aware of the feelings she had about what had occurred that weekend.

Cheryl came into my office for a therapy session the Monday following the weekend in question. She said that after house hunting for the weekend, she and her friend had gone out for Mexican food. Afterwards, she had a stomachache. At first she thought it was a response to the food, but Cheryl had begun to suspect that it was really the beginning of her awareness that she was experiencing an uneasy feeling about what had gone on during the weekend. Cheryl had taken **Step One**—*she had become aware of a feeling by respecting the messages of thr body.* In Cheryl's case, her body was definitely talking to her very loudly; telling her that something was wrong. Like many people in the healing process, Cheryl's emotion showed up as a physical sensation.

By the time Cheryl had arrived in for our session, she was at **Step Two**—*she had acknowledged the feeling.* She was beginning to understand that her physical sensation was connected with an emotion she was not yet aware of.

She then moved on to **Step Three**—*getting in touch with the emotion associated with the physical symptom.* In her case, the emotion associated with the stomachache was fear—she was afraid because things were moving very fast in the relationship.

Cheryl then moved on to **Step Four**. *She talked about it to someone she trusted.*

She realized that the emotion she was experiencing was fear. As a result of acknowledging this, she moved on to **Step Five**. *She connected the emotion in the present with something that had happened earlier.* She was not ready to live with this man. She had trust issues to resolve in connection with her father, which had been repeated many times later on in her experiences with men. Now she was able to make the connection between early trust issues and current trust issues.

As a result of making that connection, she moved on to **Step Six**—*she made a distinction between the present and the past.* When people superimpose emotion from their past onto current relationships, problems result. The intensity of early emotions is in fact a separate issue from the current experience in the present relationship, but it makes the present emotions seem more intense.

Cheryl went on to **Step Seven**—*she saw the present situation more clearly* without her history running interference.

She then moved on to **Step Eight**—*she talked about her discomfort.* The relationship was moving too fast for her, and she told this man how she felt. This led to better communication between them, because she was being honest about how she was really feeling. She was not ready to move into a house with this man.

As a result of talking about her feelings, she moved on to **Step Nine**—*she connected her stomachache with the situation.* As a result, the physical symptom went away.

This technique is helpful to break through some of the numbness experienced by the person who is healing. The numbness was there for a good reason—to protect the person from pain—and yet sometimes, the numbness does not serve a useful purpose. As in Cheryl's case, sometimes a person really wants to be close to another person, only to find that there is something blocking the way. The block is numbness.

An exercise like the one I described Cheryl going through encourages a person to stay aware of their body while experiencing emotions. This is an alternative to disowning the emotions or denying them. When we deny emotions, the body stores the emotion and remembers it, just as a computer remembers a software program stored in its memory. When deep emotions are stored in this way, medical symptoms can occur. Sometimes they are serious.

I have worked with many people who have undergone large numbers of surgeries. One woman had a history of twenty-eight surgeries, all of which involved her reproductive organs. In several cases, the surgeries could uncover no physical reason for her recurrent, severe pain. When she finally remembered portions of her childhood, however, it became clear to her that she was an incest survivor. The more she worked on memory retrieval and healing in general, the less she experienced physical pain and symptoms. Finally, her physical condition improved so much that she was able to gradually discontinue medication she had been taking for years.

In therapy, she had remembered the repeated physical, sexual abuse she had received. The memories that were stored in her body were finally released and she experienced a chance to live free of pain. Much of the pain she felt had been produced by the physical, emotional and spiritual insult of the incest.

This case is just one example of how the mind and body are connected. When people deny emotional pain they will feel and experience it in some other way. In Cheryl's case much of the memory returned through her dreams so we spent many sessions working with her dreams.

Another woman who is an incest survivor experienced a problem that happens with some frequency for incest survivors in recovery. She complained of difficulty falling asleep and getting proper rest. One night she woke up suddenly and thought she was having a heart attack. Her pulse racing, she went to the Emergency Room, where doctors gave her cardiac drugs and took an electro-cardiogram. They could find nothing wrong with her physically other than a very high pulse.

Later, in therapy, it became apparent that she had been experiencing a memory of the sexual abuse that had started very early in her life and continued on through grade school. She had had a kind of panic attack in her sleep as the memory surfaced during her dream state. This was her "heart attack."

The abuser was her grandfather. The memory caused her so much emotional pain and terror that her pulse had shot up to 160. Once she realized what had caused her "heart attack" and her sleep disorder, she was able to overcome the problems she had in getting needed rest.

Examples abound where people experience abuse memories through the messages of the body. When I talked about nightmares in an earlier chapter, I mentioned that they can be an extreme method taken by the psyche to make us pay attention. Sometimes physical symptoms are also extreme attempts by the psyche to get us to pay attention through the mechanism of a physical illness. Just as a deer runs from its predator a person's adrenal response and fight or flight reaction turn on in response to fear. Then response can be changed over time in therapy.

As people progress in recovery to Stage IV and beyond, they become very sensitive physically. It is not unusual to hear people at this stage report that they cannot get away with abusing their bodies at all anymore. Even coffee and sugar can be too much for a body and psyche that are in sync and finely tuned. Refinements in the areas of nutrition and body awareness continue through all stages. The instrument of the body becomes more finely tuned with time, until it is like a high performance race car which can only run optimally with the best of care.

Nonverbal Approaches to Healing

Words have limitations when it comes to healing. This is especially true for people who are cut off from full awareness of their bodies. In fact, sometimes it is apparent that all the talk in the world will not be enough. Fortunately, people can use nonverbal approaches to healing to help the body and mind work together in the healing process.

1. Hypnosis—Either learning self-hypnosis or going to a qualified licensed therapist who uses hypnosis can be helpful. No approach is a panacea, but hypnosis can help to get the mind and body to work in sync. Learning to focus attention in the present is what learning hypnosis is all about; it is also what learning to be comfortable in your own body is all about. The most effective hypnosis for trauma involves a combination of behavior and cognitive therapy with the hypnosis.

2. Body Work—There are licensed professionals who are trained in different body work approaches. Some work with musculoskeletal systems, others with body energy. Still others help retrieve memories and emotions with physical therapy. This can be helpful for people who want to make a connection between body, mind, emotion and spirit.

3. Art Therapy—Art, another nonverbal approach, goes beyond the defenses to reach to the emotions, and often memories as well.

4. Dance/Movement Therapy—These deal directly with the physical body. Teachers who have training in the area of dance and movement and how they connect with a person's inner life and self concept can be helpful in encouraging the healing process.

5. Sand Play Therapy—In this therapy, toys and symbols are used to experience internal reality nonverbally.

If you are a person who recalls little of their childhood but who wants to remember, the nonverbal approach to healing can help. Also, if you are a person who often blanks out when someone asks you how you feel, nonverbal therapies can help you connect the body and the emotions.

It is a gradual process to learn to be aware of and to trust your body during healing. It is always a worthwhile pursuit, because our bodies are precious—each of us only has one. Treat it well and it will return the favor.

Spirituality, Creativity, and the Healing Process

"Free will is the ability to do gladly that which I must do." C. J. Jung

The word "spirituality" has become problematic for many people. Part of this is because the word "spirit" has often been mixed in with other concepts. When I use the word in this chapter I will stick closely to the dictionary definition: "A pervading, animating principle." The word actually derives from the Latin "Spirare," meaning "to breathe." Spirit, then, is the very breath of life. It is the life force that keeps us animated, alive, and excited about being here on earth.

Being excited about being alive is something not everyone feels. People who are in early recovery feel that excitement intermittently. This is natural when people is make a major shift in their whole lifestyle. For some people, the excitement of being alive was beaten out of them at an early age—abuse and neglect affect the spirit profoundly. The spirit does not die, however. Sometimes it goes underground for years, but it can never really be destroyed.

The concept of spirit is mixed with religious ideas and images for many people. But because the spirit under discussion here is simply life force, it exists independently from any religion or philosophy.

I have worked with many people of differing religious backgrounds. Some choose not to believe in anything other than what they see in front of them, yet these people have plenty of spirit. This life principle is available to all, regardless of religious belief or disbelief.

In this chapter we will discuss the personal sense of spirit or spirituality as separate from religion. Here are some things I've learned about spirituality:

1. It is personal. Your sense of spirit is not exactly the same as anyone else's.

2. Plenty of people feel this animating life principle even though they are not religious or don't believe in a deity.

3. There is no right or wrong in how the feeling of spirit is perceived.

4. People who do not like the term "spirit," for whatever reasons, can still experience a strong sense of life force. They may call it something else, or nothing at all.

5. While the experience of spirit is personal, it is natural and universal at the same time.

6. The sense of spirit is the underlying principle behind creative experience and expression.

Factors That Block The Spirit.

The sense of spirit I'm talking about is something that nearly everyone wants. After all, it feels good. But what are the things that get in the way of experiencing this natural state? One of the major causes of damage to spirit is verbal or physical abuse suffered as a child. All child abuse is damaging, but certain types of abuse are particularly damaging to spirit. I'll discuss these first, and then offer some things that can be done about them.

Sexual abuse. Men and women who were sexually abused as children suffer damage on many levels. The most profound wounding may be that which is done to the spirit. Sexuality itself is the sharing of a person's being. It is personal and individual; it helps people define who they are. To invade human beings sexually, therefore, is to invade their spirit.

The following story illustrates both the damage and the rebirth process in recovery of the spirit of a sexual abuse survivor.

Martha came to therapy about three years after reading a book about incest and recovery; she was just beginning to experience memory recall. Her grandfather had sexually abused her over a period of several years.

Martha is a successful, professional woman. When she began therapy, she was in a relationship with a loving, caring man for the first time in her life. Yet she felt ashamed because of the abuse, and needed to work on feeling worthy of her husband's love. She also needed to work on connecting with other women—she had felt disconnected most of her life, and it was apparent that a foundation for feeling good about herself as a woman needed to be built.

Her mother was a weak woman who never protected Martha; this set the climate for her abuse. As Martha worked on her sadness and anger toward her mother in therapy, she let go of her self-contempt for her own womanhood. This emotional separation from her mother made Martha able to experience a deep love and respect for herself and other women. Now she can connect with women emotionally.

Martha worked very hard in therapy. She also read a lot of books and listened to tapes on various aspects of recovery. In addition, one of the things that pulled Martha through was her own personal sense of spirit and creativity, which she nourished. (As mentioned earlier, creativity and spirit are connected.) Just as a plant will always turn toward the light, Martha nourished herself by bathing in the light of spirit and creativity.

One of the best things she did for herself was to become active in her creative expression. She had been interested in art for some time, and her interest really blossomed during recovery. The following piece of writing, which she wrote as part of her healing process, illustrates this:

> Martha's Story:
>
> I am an incest survivor. My grandfather repeatedly abused

me from the ages of four through nine. My father is most likely a sex addict and an alcoholic; my mother is a love addict. I am a recovering love addict and have issues around compulsive eating. I have been in recovery for a little under two years now and have moved from feeling completely worthless to feeling that I'm not enough. Lately my bouts with feeling inadequate have become less and less frequent.

I have spent most of my life ignoring my gifts as a woman. I have succeeded in a man's world with very few role models. I have been a pioneer and a mentor for other women and I have done it all without giving myself credit for being a woman. I view my mother as very weak, helpless, and smothering, and have been afraid to recognize female traits within myself for fear of becoming like her. I have given my male energy all the credit for my outward successes in life. In the past year I have participated in a few (extremely safe) women's groups. My participation was very tentative at first and I still cringe sometimes about being associated with a "women's group." I have participated in these groups in spite of these feelings and always emerge feeling better about myself and the world in general. I realize now that I have been trying to reach my feminine power, to discover what it really is, and to honor and claim it as my own. This search culminated in an incredible breakthrough a few weeks ago, in a silk painting workshop in which I experienced the power of the Goddess.

This is no ordinary art class. This is the coming together of women and ancient rituals. Our work is supervised by the powers of the universe, of the gods and goddesses and of the four directions, as we honor ourselves and paint from our depths.

My first piece started as a sketch inspired by a photograph of women's heads in a Guatemalan market place. I sketched their hats, the tops of their heads, and their patterned robes. And then, seemingly out of nowhere, the Goddess appeared on the paper. I drew her with my own hands, but surely I was guided, as I have never before drawn a human figure. I drew her with the energy of the universe—it flowed from the center of the earth, up through the soles of my feet, to my heart, right out to my pencil! I felt powerful, whole, and connected to something greater than myself. I was in awe of what I had drawn, and knew that something magical had just taken place. It was a spiritual experience; I truly felt connected to the universal life force. I had experienced the power of the Goddess' energy, and my life had changed. It would take me a few weeks to recognize that I had emerged—not only an artist, but a full-fledged woman. This piece, which will soon hang in my office, has been titled "Awakenings."

Another piece was a miracle as well. Its inspiration came to me on one of my morning walks—it is a long scarf with the Goddess at the top, towering over the women of the marketplace. At this point I envisioned the women symbolically by their hats only, as in the first painting. However, when I started drawing, I thought that they should not be anonymous—they deserved faces. Once again, armed with my pencil and my Goddess energy, I ventured into unexplored territory and the faces of beautiful women emerged!

I ran into difficulty when I started to paint this piece. Some of my resist lines were so thin they were unable to contain the dyes. My carefully designed details were vanishing before my eyes. This is considered failure by one conditioned to paint (and live) within the lines. I wanted to discard this failure and begin again, doing it perfectly and fully controlled this time. But after evaluating my alternatives (scrapping the piece, reinforcing the lines, painting it anyway) and with some class encouragement, I decided that I didn't have anything to lose by continuing on and painting the piece as it was (i.e. imperfect). I must admit, however, that to appease my "within the lines" doctrine I started by painting from the bottom, the section where the line held.

As I migrated to top of the scarf, the Goddess section, I got the idea to paint flames around her head. The lesson of the broken line was joyously rewarded. What a free feeling! And what beauty emerged! I could not have planned it any better. The scarf is alive with the energy of the universe. Another

> piece of my creativity has been unleashed. The next morning on my walk, I skipped down the center of the road instead of dutifully walking down the correct side.
>
> This piece, which I have titled "Miraculous Conception," is a metaphor for the self. It has imperfections, yet it is still magnificently beautiful. Some areas are contained, and some are free-flowing. I can't love one section without loving all of them, and the whole is definitely greater than the parts.
>
> Working through this piece was like working through life. Life does not always go as we plan it, but when we have the courage to let go of specifying the outcome, we receive not what we think we wanted, but exactly what we need, which really is a much greater gift.
>
> Bless this Goddess! May I always tap into her power. May she be there to guide me along my path. May she show me the internal light of myself and lead me to believe that, yes, I truly am worth loving.

In Martha's story she beautifully described her healing process. As we have seen, although the details of the healing process vary from person to person, the theme is natural and universal, predictable and developmental. Martha used a number of supports in her healing. Therapy, reading, support groups, and art were all critical.

It was no accident that Martha's creative process really took off in recovery. In Stage III particularly, creativity often blossoms. The ability to express what is going on internally during healing is personally beneficial, and is often the basis for strong creative work. Art, writing, music, or any other creative outlet is essential to healing.

Sometimes people surprise themselves with their own creativity; it is one of the many benefits to undertaking a healing process. Another huge benefit is the enhanced sense of spirit and interest in life that is found during healing.

Of course, there are low periods, too. Facing painful memories is no fun, but while a descent into the past and the pain is necessary, it does not last forever. People who choose a healing path do not return to the past to be stuck in it. They return because a gaping wound needs attention. Sometimes the emotional and spiritual wound feels so raw that the wounded may find it surprising that people can pass them on the street and not seem to notice. If it were a physical wound, the equivalent amount of damage might alarm them enough to rush you to the emergency room, but an emotional wound is not so apparent to casual observers.

In Stage II and III, the "cleaning and dressing" of the emotional wound occurs, and going back to the past is part of it. That is why Stage II recovery is called deepening. People slowly dive into the past, deep into their own psyche. This underground journey is part of the human experience; like the winter season, it is a time to slow down and go within. Spring comes in time, and new growth of spirit and creativity then come forth.

Critical Windows in The Recovery Process and the Emergence of Creativity.

The healing process often presents itself in the form of depression—sometimes quite a deep depression. This process appears to bear a similarity to the "midlife crisis," although many people who experience it are not chronologically at midlife. They can be any age while experiencing this developmental milestone of healing. It is part of the grieving process experienced at Stage III.

As an example, most recovering people report having the feeling that, although they have been sober for several years, something is still missing: "Yes, I'm sober, but so what?" Why don't I feel good about myself or my life at a deeper level?" or "Why are my relationships falling apart?" "Why is my life lacking in meaning for me?"

I experienced a period in my own life that corresponded to this critical window in healing. Through this upheaval in my internal life, however, I noticed many gifts. One of the gifts was that the world began to slow down. Like many grieving people, I was not able to use my usual defenses—one of my defenses was work. Because I was moving and thinking more slowly, I had to cut down my work considerably.

This was frightening to me at first, as it is for many people who have this experience. But it often turns out to be a gift for the person who is willing to look inside and deal with the inner turmoil rather than try to cover it over with some habit like immersing herself in work.

A surrender that follows this experience, because it is an emotional bottom. We are alienated from ourselves, and this critical window in the Stage of Connectedness is an opportunity for a person to face the self.

When people experience this profound encounter with the self and choose not to run away, they can benefit on many levels. For instance, the creativity in a person's life can greatly increase. (When I mention this type of creativity, I mean living from moment to moment. Being fully present emotionally is truly living a creative life.) People who are willing to experience an encounter with themselves at a deep level during this time in their healing experience a growth in creativity.

I often share a myth with people who are facing this stage in their healing process. It is the myth of Atalanta. Atalanta was a goddess who was often associated with Artemis. She was widely acclaimed as a fleet-footed runner who took great pride in her ability to outdistance anyone in competition. One day a mortal man had the audacity to challenge Atalanta. Though she was insulted by this man's challenge, she went ahead and agreed to the race.

I think some kind of cosmic trickster must have been involved, because Atalanta was faced with an obstacle she had never dealt with before. She was presented with several distractions during the course of the race: three golden apples were placed strategically on her path, and she had the choice as to whether to bend down and pick them up or leave them there. The race began. The first golden apple placed before her was an apple that represented slowing down at mid-life. Atalanta looked at the apple and found it very attractive, so she paused long enough to pick it up. She then continued the race and caught up to her competitor.

After a while, she came upon the second golden apple, which represented the need to love and to be loved. For a split second she was tempted to go on, but instead she bent down and picked up the apple. Now she was beginning to have trouble keeping pace with her contestant. Finally, the third apple appeared. This apple represented the need to create. Atalanta surrendered and picked up the apple, losing the race as a result.

Although she lost the race, she won something else that was of greater value to her. She won the ability to have a meaningful relationship with herself and with another person. The price she paid was that of becoming mortal; she lost her status as a goddess.

I feel that these gifts—the ability to slow down and appreciate life, the need to love and be loved, and the need to create—are being presented to the person who is willing to take the critical window of the third stage of recovery to heart and work with it.

We can use many tools to enhance the journey through the third stage of recovery so that the person emerges richer than ever. I believe that the ability to visualize is enhanced during this stage, which is one of the most powerful tools in the healing process and in the development of creativity. In my own journey, I used visualization as a tool, developing it to the point where abilities I thought were lost to me since childhood reemerged. My visual spatial sense and color sense became enhanced. As a result, I became involved in artistic creation for the first time since my teenage years. I also did an inventory of my creativity throughout my life and determined that in a lot of ways, my artistic creativity had been suppressed by my family. I began to sculpt out of stone. This was a direct result of working with my own inner child, embracing her, and developing a relationship with her so that she could express herself artistically.

This inventory was very cleansing; and I have noticed that people who undertake such an inventory receive many benefits. It is a kind of housecleaning wherein we are able to discard old ideas about ourselves and our abilities to create.

The process of taking inventory also helps to identify shame. The more we identify shameful patterns and focus on shame reduction, the better we are able to develop new patterns that are not only healthy, but also empowering to the creative process.

As I have worked with people in this stage of recovery over the years, I have noticed that actual perceptual changes occur that support artistic expression. People see the world differently and are able to express their new perceptions, often through artistic endeavors. Another major change that occurs for people who have undergone this kind of healing process is that their passion for living returns. They experience a real interest in being alive and appreciating each new day, sometimes for the first time in the person's life. Healing becomes multidimensional, like a sculpture. Life is no longer flat and gray; it becomes full and rich.

A story about Michelangelo applies to creativity and the recovery process: One day, Michelangelo was pushing a stone slab down the street. His neighbor asked why he worked so hard over a piece of rock. Michelangelo replied, "Because there is an angel in this block that wants to come out." I believe that this third stage of recovery is an opportunity for people to let their real selves emerge. They learn to drop the false self by chipping away at it, eventually freeing the true self for creative expression in the world.

A person's inner life becomes richer as healing deepens and continues. Guidance is often presented to the person during dreams or meditation. Lisa's story illustrates this:

> During meditation I had the following experience:
>
> I was floating in a boat down a peaceful river. When the boat came to a stop I was in a bright, sunny, hilly pasture of white daisies. There was an old dilapidated barn off in the distance. An elderly plump man in overalls with a gray beard helped me out and gave me a big hug. He knew my question, and in jest assured me that I was much too naive and undeveloped within to embark upon such a demanding task as commitment with another human being. 'Learn to commit to oneself first,' he said. I said, 'But I need someone to love me and hug me.' He said, 'My child, you can learn to do all of these

things for yourself, and that will be the greatest pleasure. Once you know them for yourself, then it will be time to share; there is no hurry.'"

After the meditation, Lisa said, "I felt very relieved from the message, and I knew deep down inside of me that it was the truth. I have yet to come in contact with this guide in my meditation again. I am still trying to implant this message into a permanent place within myself."

Ethical/Moral Development and Healing

Recently, a lot of attention has been paid to the "inner child," that can be helpful in the healing process. A parallel process occurs in childhood emotional development: they grow ethically and morally as well. Not much has been written about this in the books that discuss the "inner child," but when people become stunted emotionally because they were wounded in their childhood, their ethical/moral development can become arrested as well. Here are two examples of misguided moral belief systems that some people keep well into adulthood:

Self-Blame. A forty-year-old woman who was sexually abused by her grandfather as a young child says, "I guess it was my fault. I brought it on myself." An objective observer can see that children cannot bring this on themselves. Yet it is typical of a child to believe that it was his or her fault. Any parent knows that small children think they are the center of the world. However, any adult with this type of belief would do well to reexamine it.

One thing you can do about this is to make a list of beliefs you hold. Make sure you are really honest with yourself—sit down and examine your beliefs carefully. You will probably find quite a few irrational beliefs. They would make sense to a little child; they were probably decisions you made about the world when you were a child. But some of them may be holding you back now. You can change this if you wish. Identifying them is the first step.

The Original Lie. A few years ago, I was interviewed for a Bill

Moyers show called "The Truth about Lies." We discussed the nature of lies—all kinds of lies, from societal lies to family and individual lies. I had developed an idea over the years that people often tell themselves a lie early on in childhood in order to survive painful family situations. They make that lie part of their belief system, eventually forgetting that it is a lie.

For example, a woman named Cynthia once told me a story of an event that happened to her when she was about four years old. Her father turned to her and asked her whom she loved better, him or her mother. So, at four years of age, Cynthia had a big decision to make. It was apparent to Cynthia that her father was lacking something, or he wouldn't have asked a question like that. Cynthia made a decision that from then on she would pretty much have to take care of herself, because certainly her father was too absorbed in his own problems to be able to do so.

It also became apparent to Cynthia—even at the ripe old age of four—that she was going to have to give her father an answer to that question that would keep him happy. The answer that she gave him caused her a lot of pain because it was not true; she answered, "I love you the most, Daddy." She answered this way because she knew it would make him happy, and it did. This was her original lie. In time she came to believe it, and it became a source of deep shame later on.

This is an example of how children learn to tune out their own internal messages about what the truth inside themselves is, and instead to tune in to the approval or disapproval of other people around them who are necessary for their survival. Cynthia had learned to scan the face of her father very closely, listen to his vocal intonation very carefully, and give him answers that would make him happy—she wanted to make him smile and make his voice sound pleased and not angry. She learned this lesson so well that she became an expert at reading other people's emotions and keeping them happy. These skills certainly helped her in some respects, but they held her back in the area of becoming intimate. In order to become intimate with another person, we have to know ourselves first. And she was such an expert at tuning in to other people that she really had no idea of who she was.

It is worth taking the time to identify any original lies you may have told yourself to survive as a child. As part of this, you can list the beliefs you were taught by your family and decide which ones you wish to keep in adulthood. Then list the beliefs that you have been living out in your life. Decide which of these you want to keep. Finally, decide which beliefs and values are high priorities for you.

Some beliefs cannot be compromised. For instance, for a recovering alcoholic, believing in the need to stay sober has to be #1 on the priority list. If it is any lower on the list, the commitment to sobriety is not strong enough, and relapse is a possibility.

This process encourages self-honesty. Any original lies you told yourself about who you were in order to survive will surface. You can then empower yourself by choosing, as an adult, what you believe about yourself and what are your own values, attitudes and beliefs.

Relationships and Sexuality during the Healing Process

Here are some of the questions that people who were raised in dysfunctional families ask about healthy relationships:

> "Will I recognize a healthy relationship—would I recognize one if it was right in front of me?"
> "Is there such a thing as a healthy relationship? I don't know anybody who's in one."
> "If I were in a healthy relationship, would it be so boring that I couldn't stay in it?"
> "Will I ever stop feeling this despair and hopelessness about relationships?"
> "How do you tell if a relationship is healthy?"

One of the many miracles of the healing process is that as people begin to get healthy, they begin to recognize the relative level of health of other people in their lives as well. As they recognize this, they begin to gravitate toward and attract healthier people into their lives. But a healthy relationship starts at home, so to speak, with oneself, so I will first cover having a healthy relationship with yourself and then discuss having a healthy relationship with a partner or mate.

Acceptance and Love

A woman named Beth who was a patient of mine some years ago told me a story that I will never forget. When she was about seven or eight years old she habitually got on her bicycle and travel for about five miles down the road to visit some neighbors. These neighbors were a large Filipino family with ten children, and Beth wanted to spend as much time as she possibly could with this family. Although she had little in common with this family socially, economically, or culturally, Beth sensed some quality about their home life that she really gravitated toward. In describing the several years of her childhood during which she visited this family, tears would come to her eyes, even thirty years afther the fact. She described the parents, the love they had for each other, and how it extended out toward their children and all the people they knew.

I asked her if there was love in her family and she said yes, she believed that her parents loved her, although her family had many problems. Beth's father was an active alcoholic during her childhood; he has since become sober, but she still remembers his drinking days.

When she described the love in her own family, she became puzzled—something was still missing in her family, even though love was present. It wasn't just the alcoholism in and of itself that had made things unpleasant at home; it was some other quality that still eluded her. As a matter of fact, the absence of this quality was one of the things that brought her to therapy in the first place. She was motivated to come to therapy because she felt a lack of intimacy with her husband—that quality was missing in her marriage of many years. She loved her husband just as she loved her parents and they loved her, but there was something missing. This missing element was a theme running through her life.

As we talked more and I learned more about her history and her current problem, I asked her if she saw any difference between love and acceptance. She thought for a while, looked puzzled, and said, "I thought love and acceptance were the same thing—aren't they?" I said that I didn't think love and acceptance were the same thing, that I saw love in many families, even very troubled families. But in those same families there was also a lack of acceptance. Her face lit up and she said, "Yes, that was the quality that was missing at home—I never really felt accepted at home. I always felt that I had to do something or get the right grades or look the right way or say the right thing to keep my parents happy, and then they would love me. But I never felt I was just accepted for myself; I never really felt listened to. I never felt my parents were just there for me without making any judgments or any demands that I perform in some way. When I visited this Filipino family, I felt that the parents really accepted each other and their children, and that acceptance would be there whether they performed well or not."

Beth's story illustrates that a family can be loving without being accepting. To accept another person, you must first accept yourself as you are with all the human flaws. This is the basis of self-forgiveness in healing, and it blossoms; in full flower, this quality becomes self-love. The greater the self-acceptance, the more a person can accept others with all their human flaws. This wholeness is the basis for real love and commitment.

The inventory process that I described earlier in this book is the cornerstone of self-acceptance. Becoming aware of one's strengths and weaknesses as a human being is the beginning of self-acceptance as well as the basis for true humility. That we are no better or worse than anybody else is a natural and universal principle. Forgiveness comes with more ease when we have this knowledge, and forgiveness is an essential component in a committed relationship.

The Fragmented Self

People inevitably bring their internal restlessness and sense of inner fragmentation into their adult relationships.

In many homes, this fragmentation occurs because it was dangerous to develop an integrated personality while growing up. People become fragmented in order to survive—it is a normal response to an abnormal amount of stress and pain in childhood. In the Chapter on Stage 4 of the healing process, Integration, I talked about the meaning of the word "integration" in some depth. Humans naturally seek a kind of wholeness, just as a plant grows toward the light. It is natural to want to feel whole, and the healthier you get while healing, the more you will notice that fragmented parts of your personality still exist. This does not mean that you are regressing, it only means that you are becoming more aware of yourself.

There is no simple, snap answer to this problem. I have noticed that healing brings with it a sense of wholeness in and of itself. When you are truly aware of this kind of fragmentation, it becomes unacceptable to you, and your behavior changes as a result. People reduce the fragmentation in their outer world as a reflection of inner awareness.

Internal Restlessness

A sense of internal restlessness is usually coupled with a deep feeling of loneliness and emptiness. People who grew up in homes where family members exhibited a lot of inconsistent behavior are bound to end up feeling restless later on in their intimate relationships. Children need to have a predictable, consistent environment; when they are not provided with it, they become internally restless. Later on in adult life, this internal restlessness continues and produces a constant need for attention and entertainment, as well as a fear of boredom. (I define the word "boredom" as lack of awareness, so that when you are feeling that kind of internal restlessness, ask yourself what is really going on inside you. What feelings are you having? Boredom is not a real feeling—it is a cover-up for a kind of anxiety and a genuine feeling underneath it. Take the time to identify what you are really feeling.)

Sometimes people are uncomfortable being in their own homes, often due to unpleasant memories of things that happened at home as a child, including abuse. Are you uncomfortable in your home—do you have a constant need to be entertained by having the TV or radio on all the time? This is often a sign of internal restlessness. It will wane with time and growing self-awareness in recovery. When you are more comfortable being alone, relationships with others will be more satisfying. They will be based on caring rather than a need for a distraction.

Waiting for Life to Occur

People who grew up in chaotic families often had to wait to get their needs met, and a feeling of anxiety accompanies this waiting. Often they were waiting for the other shoe to drop, so to speak. There was a high degree of tension, and because of that tension, coupled with the inconsistency in how they would be treated, they could never be sure what was going to happen next. At any moment a disaster could occur, or a drama could unfold that would be completely out of their control.

This pattern of waiting for the other shoe to drop often carries through to adulthood and intimate relationships, and a person may retain a lot of anxiety. Even when things are going well in an adult relationship, the person may feel a sense of discomfort, as if something bad is going to happen at any moment. Identifying this as an old pattern from childhood that does not necessarily apply in adulthood is a very powerful thing to begin to change the pattern.

Part of this pattern is a feeling that if only one particular magical thing would happen, life would be wonderful. For example, "If only I could lose nineteen pounds, my life would be perfect," or "If only I had that job or that car, then life would be great."

Clearly, a pattern can be established in early childhood of waiting for things to happen. Whether they are good things or bad things, the pattern is putting life on hold. If you are experiencing a pattern like this, be aware that acknowledging it will help you break it. It is a sad thing to see people waste their lives waiting and waiting when they can prevent this. People who experience a lot of pain early in life often make bargains with themselves that they will wait until a particular age and things will be better because they will be on their own or they will be married, with their own families. But this is a kind of bargaining that can rob people of their own lives if it continues. You have the power to identify it and stop it now.

Is It Success or Love that I'm After?

People from deeply wounded families often learn to work very hard toward recognition, achievement, and respect. These are all positive qualities, but they are not the same as love. Because people want love, they confuse it with respect and success. Many people get depressed even though they are successful in their business or professional lives, because that success does not translate into being loved. Learn to separate these two things in your mind because it is important to recognize and accept love on its own. A workaholic pattern can be rooted in a fear that love is something that can be taken away at any given time. In the end, people who seek respect and achievement without attending to their need to give and express love are very much alone.

Recapturing Innocence

People who are in the early stages of healing need to work to recapture innocence. This is particularly true of people who were sexually abused as children. Often a period of celibacy in adulthood is a good preparation for a committed relationship later on. During this time people can work on their own healing, which takes time and energy.

Romantic Obsessions

In early healing stages people often experience romantic obsessions before they are ready to be involved in a relationship. In a sense, these obsessions are like a drug—they serve as a distraction. Often the obsessions involve people who are unavailable for a relationship because they are already married or of a different sexual persuasion. The lack of availability in and of itself keeps the person in early recovery safe from being involved with another person.

A woman named Robin told me of her experience with dating in early recovery:

> "As I began to restructure my existence within therapy, AA, and daily contact with my higher power, I began to have a

> desire to date. But I was morally bankrupt, and had no conception of how to enter into this new experience with men. It was new because now I was sober. I was very afraid, but once I started dating I realized I was falling back to my crazy thinking about falling in love, marrying, and having children with every man I dated.
>
> I think this is my biggest challenge right now, to get my thoughts and my behaviors straightened out. I have learned to try to listen to my gut feelings and to realize that my brain is still very sick and naive. My emotional maturity is about fifteen years old. I know in my rational mind that I am not emotionally capable of entering a committed relationship at this time, even though my heart is full of lust and I crave a man. It would not only be extremely harmful for me but for the other person as well. So I must learn to be honest, I must learn unconditional love, and I must become capable of thinking in an adult way. The only way I have found to honestly pursue my innermost knowledge of myself is to know the 'presence' within me and rely on my higher power to guide me into the contemplation of my decisions. I work daily on my meditations."

At this point, Robin was about nine months sober. She was still in her first year of sobriety, but we can see that she was making a lot of progress in terms of her self-awareness, and this in turn extended to some changes in her behavior with regard to men. She still caught herself obsessing and fantasizing about each man she dated, but she didn't have the desire to become engaged or to marry them, as she had in the past. Also, she was not bingeing on food anymore, as she used to do when she would feel the stress of a romantic relationship that was becoming closer.

Seen for what it is—a transient or a temporary condition to be learned from—we can examine romantic obsessions just as Robin did.

"Will You Be Back?"—Separation Is Different from Abandonment

People who confuse separation with abandonment run into a lot of painful situations in their adult intimate relationships. Separation in a healthy adult-to-adult relationship is an agreed-upon period of time during which people are on their own, with the understanding that the two people will eventually get together again.

Abandonment occurs when a person simply disappears from your life. Abandonment is connected with childhood fear and pain. Even a parent who is physically present can emotionally abandon a child through inconsistent parenting. It is hard for a child to understand the difference between separation and abandonment. But as we grow up, we begin to make a distinction between the two. Not all separations equal abandonment.

Adults who are in intimate relationships need to know that they are not necessarily being abandoned because a separation occurs. It is all right to ask people with whom you are close when they are coming back. Let them know that you have needs. Asking for clarity is appropriate, and a very powerful tool in removing this old confusion. This kind of clear framework for understanding reduces anxiety, and it is an important tool to help you feel safe within a relationship. Remember: adults cannot be abandoned, because they have the ability to make choices in their lives that children don't have.

People in a healing process have many challenges when it comes to relationships. But in some ways, they are actually in a stronger position than others. Why? Because people who undertake a healing path and change their lives learn tools that are useful in relationships. Here are some of the tools learned through the healing process that will help you in a committed relationship:

1. How to make a commitment. People in recovery already know what a real commitment is. They have already had to make a 100 percent commitment to stay on their healing path.

2. A sense of humor. People who attend 12-Step meetings, especially AA, know that the healing process contains a considerable amount of laughter. People in recovery learn to view themselves with a certain sardonic and humble humor—an asset in relationships.

3. A strong desire to work at a relationship. It takes constant work and attention to have a loving relationship. People who are pursuing their own healing know what it is to work hard at something worthwhile.

4. The ability to forgive. When I ask couples what are the biggest factors that make a relationship work, three things come up again and again—humor, communication, and forgiveness. Forgiveness is part of the healing process; it is practiced frequently on the healing path. When we learn to forgive ourselves we can more readily forgive others.

5. Honesty. People in recovery must learn to be honest with themselves, or they will return to their old lifestyles. This honesty is essential in relationships.

6. The ability to remain friends. Start with a friendship and then, when it turns to romance, keep the friendship alive. People on a healing path learn to develop and value friendships; they are the lifeblood of success in healing.

7. The existence of a system that supports the relationship. A romantic relationship cannot flourish in isolation if it is to grow into a committed union. Just as a plant has a root system that helps feed it, friends, family and community must feed a union between two people if it is to last.

8. A cause or belief larger than yourselves. If as a couple you are involved in some type of a cause, a spiritual belief, or some activity that has meaning to both of you but is larger than either of you individually, it tends to lend a very helpful perspective. For example, couples who are involved in some kind of religious or political cause gain a perspective that the world and its problems are larger than their own. This is helpful to maintain a healthy point of view about the kind of interpersonal problems that can arise in a relationship.

9. Negotiating skills. Partners need to give each other the kind of respect that they would give a business associate or a friend. It is understood in a business negotiation that each person will have his or her say and the other party will listen, and then some compromise will be undertaken. Negotiations are often necessary in all kinds of relationships, and people who are committed to healing know this.

10. Shared values and a sense of purpose. Couples who stay together for a long period of time are generally people who have a sense of values and a shared purpose in life. It is helpful to identify what your values are by doing a values assessment. This is done by simply sitting down with a piece of paper and a pencil and making a list of the kinds of values that you were taught as a child in your family. Some of these values were probably verbalized by your parents, and some were apparent as a result of their behavior but not necessarily discussed. You can decide which of these values you are still living by as an adult. Perhaps you want to keep some of these values in your life. You may not want to keep others. In this way you will get in touch with your current values and perhaps add some new ones along the way that you aspire toward. Also, you can make a list of what your priority values are; be willing to negotiate on them. If you are in a relationship, your mate can make a similar list; then you might share your lists with one another. People who have values that are basically the same or complimentary to one another tend to do better in a long-term relationship.

11. Strong bonding rituals. Couples bond together in many ways and encourage and build those bonds through the years. There are several kinds of bonding rituals that have been studied among couples. The first ritual forms the kind of bond that is established when people greet each other or say good-bye. The second kind of bond is the recognition of certain anniversary dates and holidays, and how couples choose to celebrate those occasions together. The third kind of bonding ritual is a unique bond for any specific couple. For example, I worked with a couple who separated when the wife was in early recovery from her alcoholism. It had been a very difficult time in their marriage; when she went into recovery, they realized they still had a lot of problems as a couple. They underwent marital therapy. During this time I asked them what their bonding rituals were. As it developed, one of their primary bonding rituals was to have a barbecue on the weekends. This gave them a feeling of closeness and established a kind of intimacy and comfort between them. They reestablished this bonding ritual during their separation, and it was one of the things that helped to bridge the gap in communication that they had experienced for some time as a result of the alcoholism and recovery process. It is important for a couple to identify their own unique bonding rituals and to really honor them.

Sexuality and the Healing Process

It is not an easy task to write about sexuality these days. Sex, disease and death have become closely connected in an age where sexual decisions can have serious repercussions. But many good books have been written that deal with the subjects of AIDS and safe sex. Because they are not the topics of this book, I would refer you to them for a thorough examination of those subjects. In everything I have written here about sex, the following factors are assumed:

1. It is sex between two mutually consenting, adult partners in a committed, caring relationship.
2. The information is applicable whether it is a heterosexual or same sex union.

In books written on various aspects of recovery, the logical emphasis is on abuse and illness of one type or another. These tools are important; illness and pathology of varying types need to be explored. But because so many books are available on these topics, I will concentrate on a relatively neglected one—sexuality as a joy-giving, spirit-enhancing, healing experience.

The experience of sexuality itself undergoes changes through the recovery and healing stages. During Stage I, for example, there is a tendency to confuse anxiety with sexual feelings.

Anyone who has sat through a 12-Step meeting (especially AA) with a lot of newcomers knows that a lot of squirming in chairs, covert (and some not-so-covert) sexual surveying, and prowling goes on. There is even an expression called "the 13th step," which refers to program members becoming sexually involved with newcomers. Everyone knows—because they have been told at one time or another—that it is not a good idea to get involved in a relationship in the first year of recovery. Sometimes, however, this is said with a snicker or a leer, as if to suggest that sexual involvement is OK, but a real committed relationship is not. What this actually reveals is a sense of shame and anxiety related to sex.

Healing people of all sorts find confusion between anxiety and sexual feelings. The feeling of arousal that a person experiences when angry, anxious, or frightened is often misinterpreted at this stage as sexual arousal; this lack of a refined distinction between and among types of arousal causes a lot of problems. It is part of the reason behind the wisdom of the adage, "don't get involved the first year."

Another reason to stay away from both quick sexual involvement and new commitment during this first year is the need to focus on yourself. This is all most people can handle while meeting the challenges of Stage I Healing.

In addition, for those who are in early chemical dependency recovery, the body is undergoing a tremendous adjustment. There are significant physical changes, and women and men may tend to be uninterested in sex for a period of time. Men may experience difficulty achieving and maintaining an erection. Given time, however, sexual dysfunction usually proves to be transitory. (A physician should always be consulted should problems continue, but they rarely do.) In Stage I, people rarely make a connection between their physical, emotional, and spiritual beings. They are usually still cut off from themselves. Thus, an interest in sex is usually either for physical release or to chase after a fantasy or obsession, as I discussed earlier. The ability to love comes later, after self-love is learned.

By the time Stage II is reached, there is often a sense of longing for a connection. People sometimes mistake this as longing for a romantic relationship, but it is usually longing for the self—the early stirrings of self-love. In Stage II, the focus is on going into the personal emotional exploration that is the foundation of budding compassion, forgiveness, and true love.

Lots of people are in couple relationships from the beginning of their journey through healing. Not all relationships make it through. The ones that do involve two people who are willing to work at growing together. Quite a bit of patience and maturity are required.

People generally get involved in a relationship because they are at about the same level of personal growth and maturity. If they continue to grow at the same rate, they can expect the relationship to go well. If not, conflict occurs.

In Stage II and Stage III, people begin to make a deeper connection to their mates as they begin to connect more deeply with themselves. This has tremendous impact on sexuality. To connect emotional, spiritual, physical, and mental responses is a huge task. It is the stuff of true partnership in couples. People who used to find themselves "always interested in sex" change and become less so as they find the need to feel an emotional connection with a partner to experience satisfying sex. The psyche and the body become one, and as fragmentation becomes a thing of the past, people's standards rise higher and higher in terms of what is an acceptable sexual experience.

Sexual abuse survivors often go through a period of time when they need to establish that they are in control of their bodies. Control and safety are so closely linked that the terms are often interchangeable As a result, male and female survivors may go for months or even years of refusing to be sexually involved. This control is very important for their recovery, but it is also tough on any existing relationships—what is a companion to do all that time? There are no simple answers, but patience, true selfless love and understanding go a very long way in these situations.

Part of the healing journey for sexual abuse survivors involves the absolute need to partake in sexual contact that is:

1. Freely chosen
2. Spirit enhancing

3. Increasingly pleasurable, so they can slowly learn to experience more physical pleasure over time

4. Nonabusive or coercive

5. Under their control as to when it stops and starts

6. An experience that emphasizes the present moment

7. Nonjudgmental

8. Caring—with a loving partner

In looking at this list, I think most people would agree that these are desirable criteria for any satisfying sexual experience. Unfortunately, some cases when none of these criteria are met cause an injury that must be encouraged to heal. Here is a story told by a woman who is reclaiming her sexuality as part of her healing:

> I have always known that my grandfather routinely molested me when I was young. But my family taught me early on that anything difficult, scary, or upsetting wasn't to be talked about, so I never talked about the incest to anyone. I grew up, got a job, a husband, a house and two cars in the garage. Then, three days after the birth of my son, my life changed. I started feeling nervous—worried about everything. All the good feelings I usually had slowly left, and fear and anxiety took their place.
>
> I would look around me and find no explanation for the feelings inside—I didn't even have words to describe them. Only one thing helped, and that was alcohol. Alcohol became a daily glue, the only thing that kept me together. Eventually, I had to drink so much to keep from feeling the fear inside that alcohol became a problem in itself.
>
> I went through treatment for alcoholism, but within ten days of getting out I wanted to die. I was diagnosed as having major depression; medication and therapy two to three times a week were prescribed.
>
> It was the most painful time in my life. I felt so close to going over the edge and not knowing who I was or where I was. I was in such bad shape mentally, emotionally, and spiritu-

ally that it took a whole year before I could look back and say I had gotten better. After two years I finally felt well enough to go back to my job and a normal life. With bimonthly therapy and AA, life was tolerable.

Our daughter was born shortly after my fifths AA anniversary, and the evening after she was born I drank the champagne they served me in the hospital. That was because on the day she was born, that old fear was definitely back. I wasn't able to say "something is deadly wrong again and I don't know why again," so instead I returned to drinking. The progression talked about in the Big Book is true; after another year and a half of drinking, I was once again on my knees.

It was writing a fourth step (an Inventory) in a second treatment center when I suddenly knew what I needed to do. It became clear that speaking up about the incest was as important to me as staying sober. The two have gone hand in hand ever since—I have to heal from the incest to stay sober, and I have to stay sober to heal from the incest.

I asked four people in the program to recommend a therapist, and the same name came back all four times. That was the first of many miracles in my journey of sexual healing. It's been as painful and difficult as it has been wonderful. I've gone to a workshop and screamed and cried at empty chairs. I've gone to my abuser's grave and had a ceremony with my sister where we spoke our true memories. I've sat in my therapist's office and regressed into a small child crying and crying because she's certain she's a bad girl.

It became clear early in the therapy that I needed to take a break from sex. I had never learned how to say no. That six months of sexual abstinence put a tremendous amount of stress on my marriage, for a number of reasons. Not having sexual relations seemed to free up a lot of pictures, memories—I relived a lot of those things I didn't know I remembered. I had to feel them, talk about them, get angry about them, cry about them, do all the things to settle with them that I couldn't do as a child. During this time I also took a leap of faith and quit the medication for depression I had been on for years. It was time to feel the feelings down to my core. This work seemed to alleviate a lot of the stuff that had made it necessary for me to mentally and emotionally "leave" during sex.

I have to be very careful now that I've resumed sexual relations not to slip back into just presenting my body for use and leaving. I've progressed from leaving my body to being emotionally present. Now I'm reaching for passion and desire. I find the more I am in charge of my sex life (the where, the when, the how) the better it feels for me. Recently I "kidnapped" my husband for his birthday and took him to a fancy hotel for the night. Making love that night was the best it had ever been for me. Somehow, surprising him and being in control made me feel sexy and grown up—real firsts for me.

When I first sat down and dared to remember, I could see the sexual and emotional wounds were huge. What I have learned since is that the spiritual wounds were just as large. As I heal sexually I heal spiritually—and the benefits are profound.

When I started I had little sense of myself or of power within. The more work I do, the more I become filled. As I learn to love this woman, I connect and get strength from all women. Dreams are beginning to return to me. I have experienced my intuition; my "knowing"; my voice. I am no longer in a black hole, not knowing what to do. When I feel anxiety and fear today, it tells me I need to take action. I'm learning what to do for myself to feel OK. When I'm feeling good today, it's so good that I want to stand up and shout, "Look at me—I'm whole!"

By the time Stage IV recovery is reached, people who have worked hard in the other stages are feeling more whole than ever before. Relationships are more likely to be built on mutual respect and affection rather than on neediness, dependency and manipulation.

Some Sexual Techniques That Can Be Healing

Many books have been written on sexual difficulties, damage, and problems. However, few books have addressed aspects of a loving sexual union that can be healing. In Western medicine and psychology, there are limitations when it comes to sexual research and information. This is because of the dominance of the scientific model in Western medicine, which is wonderful for research, but is lacking in tools to enhance the spiritual aspects of sexuality. The scientific model tends to present a dry, mechanistic perspective on sexuality. Sexuality is about much more than the physical. It is about love, energy, healing, and spirit as well. This is why the Western sex therapy model is not enough when it comes to sexual healing.

Blending what is known from the Western model with some of the knowledge from the East allows for a more complete model of sexual expression and sexual healing. Because so much of the existing material on sexual response for couples is from a Western perspective, I will not discuss that here. I will discuss other healing techniques that are thousands of years old, rarely discussed in the West, yet well known in the East.

Tantra

There are a number of books available on Tantra. Many are too esoteric to be of any great practical use to couples. However, I list one in the bibliography of this book that is specifically written for Western couples. It is a short, information-packed volume. Couples can read it together.

As I have said, sexuality is much more than a physical act. In recovery, people realize this more and more with time. Tantra takes the position that sexual love and union is nourishing to the soul. The whole concept of spirit as I have discussed it in this book is encompassed in a Tantric approach to partnership

Tantra teaches the ability to form a satisfying, spirit-enhancing sexual union that elevates the couple's relationship to an art form. This attitude is in contrast to the way many people were introduced to their own sexuality. This is especially true of people who were sexually abused, coerced and manipulated as children.

This new attitude can be learned alone or within the context of a committed relationship in which two people are willing to work and heal together. Here are some things to keep in mind:

1. Start slowly; learn to accept and appreciate your own body.

2. Focus your sexual activity on loving and on exchange of positive energy rather than on orgasm and genital pleasure alone.

3. Slow down in sexual situations. Give yourself permission to stop and start as you wish. This is particularly helpful for sexual abuse survivors who may experience a flashback during a sexual experience. Permission for a time out breaks the pattern of intrusive flashback material. (This applies to people learning to pleasure themselves alone as well as to couples.)

4. Learn to nurture one another. Affection and cuddling are important exchanges in and of themselves. Sexual abuse survivors especially need to know that they will not be seen as objects for someone's physical gratification; they will be seen as human beings first.

5. Sexuality is an art form. The word art is from Latin and translates literally as "skill." Any skill becomes better with time and practice.

6. If you have no partner, remember that everything you do that is loving toward yourself will also prepare you to love someone else more fully.

7. When we love something we spend time on it. Make time for your partner and your shared sexual pleasure.

8. Keep your eyes open and the lights on at least some of the time during a sexual experience. This will remind you to stay in present time and to be emotionally present with your partner. If you have difficulty being present, ask for a time out to communicate what is going on with you.

9. Balance giving and receiving in a sexual experience.

10. Value yourself and your gift. In Tantra, the body is consid-

ered a temple of the spirit. This means that you value your body and spirit highly. Do not ask just anyone to partake in sharing your spirit and its temple. It is a special gift.

11. Consider learning the Sacred Spot Massage. Both women and men have an area that when lovingly massaged can accelerate healing. It is called the Sacred Spot in Tantra. (In Western research it is called the Graffenberg or G-spot.) A woman can touch it herself, but it is not easy for her to reach alone. This is why it is helpful for a partner to locate the spot and massage it. The spot can be located by squatting and pressing up with two fingers inside the vagina toward the navel, while pressing down externally just along the pubic bone with the other hand. When this spot is massaged, it will swell, making it easier to feel with two sets of fingers. Because it is physically awkward to accomplish this alone, a partner can help. Massaging the spot requires a loving, gentle touch. Stimulating this spot through massage produces an awakening process which is deeply healing, because the spot holds pleasure and also memory of prior sexual experiences. Sometimes past experiences will be remembered when the spot is gently massaged; this offers an opportunity for healing past trauma. As memories are released, intense pleasure can be experienced. There is no rush—be loving and take your time.

Sometimes there is a fluid that is released when a woman's sacred spot is stimulated. This is a healing fluid called Amrita. It is a light-colored liquid similar to a man's ejaculate. Many women experience pleasure when their amrita is flowing. Some produce a few drops and some produce copious amounts.

This type of sexual massage is very intimate. Undertake it alone or with a partner that you trust and love.

Men have a sacred spot, too. Theirs can be massaged as well. It is located at the slight indentation on the perineum, midway between the testicles and the anus. It can be gently massaged as well for the same reason and with the same result as the female massage.

12. Be open to exercises that increase sexual response and con-

trol. Both men and women can benefit from pelvic muscle-strengthening exercises. Women benefit because these exercises strengthen their vaginal muscles, often making intercourse more pleasurable for them and their orgasms stronger. Men benefit because they can learn ejaculatory control and achieve stronger, firmer erections. Increased ejaculatory control also means that men can learn to separate ejaculation and orgasm—they are not the same. Men are capable of experiencing control over when they ejaculate and when they orgasm. They are also capable of experiencing multiple orgasm.

To strengthen the pubococcygeal muscles (PC muscles) you must locate them first. For both men and women, they are the muscle group used in stopping urination mid-stream, by clenching. If the muscle is weak, this may be difficult to accomplish. But like any other muscle, it can be strengthened by use and practice. You can exercise your PC muscles anywhere, simply by doing this clenching exercise. As the PC muscles gain strength, you will be able to distinguish them from other muscles.

A man who strengthens this muscle can begin to feel orgasmic sensation earlier. As a result, he can clench the muscle in order to prolong making love, thus reversing the flow. This, combined with stopping all movement and breathing deeply, can teach ejaculatory control with practice.

All of the techniques mentioned above require two things. One is a caring partnership where both individuals want healing for one another; the other is open and frequent communication during sexual experiences.

Partners can go a long way toward healing each other, and thus soar above their past histories. Sexual loving used as a tool in this way can be an emotional and spiritual bonding, bringing a couple to new heights through their union.

Conclusion

Turning Wounds into Gifts for the Individual, Family, and Society

There is an old saying, sometimes used in comedy routines—"it's all done with mirrors." For me it always brings to mind a physician I knew many years ago who conducted his medical practice out of his home from an iron lung. When a patient came to see this doctor, the patient was instructed by the doctor's assistant—his devoted wife—to stand in a particular spot and to turn at a special angle in order for the doctor to examine the patient through a reflected image from a series of mirrors that were attached to the iron lung. This doctor was an allergist and a skin specialist, but mostly what he did was listen. He was very good at listening, and gave recommendations in a voice that sounded a lot like that of Lionel Barrymore when he played Doctor Gillespie in the old Doctor Kildare movies of the 1940s. In this doctor's mind, the patient might detail a litany of physical and emotional wounds, but his job was to listen. People opened up to this doctor as if he were a priest or a psychiatrist. There was something in his manner that was very accepting; he had a quality of suspending judgment about people and situations that encouraged openness.

This doctor handed down a legacy of medicine and healing—his son is presently practicing medicine in the same community. All families hand down legacies to their children, their children's children and beyond. Some of these legacies are gifts that the children receive; some of them are wounds, but wounds can be turned into gifts with awareness and growth. A lot of the material in this book is about turning wounds into gifts. At this point I'd like to talk about the kinds of wounds that are developed into gifts with the help of families and communities.

We all need to think about the legacy we are leaving to our children, their children, and their children's children. What kind of a world do we want? Do we want a world that is like a macrocosm of one of the music concerts I described in the first chapter of this book? If so, which one—the chaotic Altamont event or the peaceful Sedona concert? Can we choose, or is it too late?

I prefer to think that it is not too late—that we can still turn things around. Hope is the feeling that what we desire is also possible, and I believe that a peaceful world is possible. Of the two concerts, I choose Sedona. I choose hope.

To leave this legacy to our children, a healing change must take place. Where does it start? It already has. Every time a person feels that internal shift, recognizes that moment as a state of grace, takes action and starts to heal, we all heal.

The profound change people experience when they make a 100 percent commitment to heal is something other people see mirrored in their eyes. We all thirst for that state of grace, for that spirit to fill the void deep inside ourselves.

Hope is a contagious condition. It spreads faster than any disease I know of. An individual who feels hope spreads it to friends, family members, co-workers, and the community. Millions of people are deciding to make that change. They, in turn, are affecting millions of others exponentially.

Families and communities undergo a natural, universal, developmental, and predictable healing process that parallels that of the individual healing stages discussed in this book. When the numbers of individuals undergoing a healing and recovery process are big enough, society is shaken. This is happening right now. Families are shaken at first, then transformed by members who choose a healing path. These families are never the same again. Old roles begin to crumble and dissolve; subjects never before discussed are openly broached. People become anxious at first, because they don't know what to expect. But then they begin to work on healing old wounds.

At first it may be so painful that things seem to be getting worse rather than better. But in Stage II and Stage III, families have faced their wounds and have sought help. They recognize their strengths and are able to learn about the nature of true love and compassion. In Stage IV, families regroup as new, more flexible systems. Interdependence is achieved.

Different families are currently at various stages of family healing, but the highs and lows that individuals within them experience are the same, and the intensity of the healing increases along with the number of family members who are working individually and together. At the community level it is no different.

So, one might ask, what are we recovering from as a whole? I believe that there is deep pain, not only in the generation of people who are in their 30s and early 40s—the baby boomers—but also in the generations that preceded and succeeded by them as well. The generation that preceded the Vietnam era was a generation of people that for the most part held dearly to very high ideals with regard to faith in family, a work ethic, and a national identity. In many cases those high ideals were coupled with a kind of blind faith that is also part of idealism, which was shattered in the post-World War II era. So the schisms within families that people point to now—today's high rate of divorce and chemical dependency—had their roots in this earlier generation's high expectations of family life; some people might say these were overly high expectations.

The Second World War produced both a tremendous cohesiveness among a generation and a tremendous need for adjustment after the war. For many families, changes took place not only because men went off to war, but also because women went to work. They were then expected to adjust to a return to a more traditional family life after the war, but this was a very difficult adjustment. So the baby boom generation inherited some of the blind faith and some questioning of basic values as a legacy of its parents.

As a result of having grown up in the depression, the parents of the baby boomers were also a generation that had a lot of questions and insecurities regarding faith in economic stability. In addition, many of them divested themselves of their cultural roots in an attempt to assimilate into American society.

These legacies had profound personal effects on individuals and families. Peace is necessary for any group to develop, and on one level peace starts with the inner peace of the individual. Many of these families experienced very little peace; in fact, a sense of restlessness was part of the legacy of the pre-war generation. It was passed down to their children and their children's children.

This sense of a deep void that was passed down through generations was rarely acknowledged or discussed. However, it still profoundly affected millions of people. It is some of this inherited pain that is at the root of the emptiness we often feel as part of the family experience today.

In the baby boom generation, many people suffered as a result of the Vietnam war and the rift that the war caused in families. Whether people served in Vietnam or refused because of conscientious objection, the effect was profound on families and on society. I have seen many instances where fathers had never met their children, and some are still being reunited with children they have never seen or have been alienated against as a result of that war.

The movement in this country toward an increased openness and an ability to acknowledge, verbalize and communicate pain is the beginning of a step toward a healthier society. Many people are coming forward because there is more permission now to do so. However, many of those who are in pain are just beginning to look at some options for handling it.

This book, then, is not only about healing for individuals; it is also about the healing of several generations of people. Families and communities are recovering a sense of hope in the future—not only hope that there will be a future, but also hope that each of us can be active and constructive participants in it. This can and will happen as a result of working for a kind of peace; this peace is fostered in the outer world at the group level, but also within the family, within society, and within our own inner worlds as well.

Bibliography

Austen, Hallie. *The Heart of the Goddess.* Berkeley: Winslow Press, 1990.

Bass, Ellen and Laura Davis. *The Courage to Heal: A Guide for Women Survivors of Childhood Abuse.* New York: Harper and Row, 1988.

Beckmann, Linda J. "Reported Effects of Alcohol on the Sexual Feelings and Behavior of Women Alcoholics and Nonalcoholics." *Journal of Studies on Alcohol* 40 (1979): 272-82.

_______. "Women Alcoholics: A Review of Social and Psychological Studies." *Journal of Studies on Alcohol* 36, no. 7 (1975): 797-824.

_______. "Self-Esteem of Women Alcoholics." *Journal of Studies on Alcohol* 39, no. 3 (1978): 491-98.

_______. "Perceived Antecedents and Effects of Alcohol Consumption in Women." *Journal of Studies on Alcohol* 41, no. 5 (1980): 518-30.

Billings, Andrew G., Marc Kessler, Christopher A. Gomber, and Sheldon Weiner. "Marital Conflict Resolution of Alcoholic and Nonalcohalic Couples during Drinking and Nondrinking Sessions." *Journal of Studies on Alcohol* 40, no. 3 (1979): 183-95.

Bly, Robert. *Iron John.* Massachusetts: Addison Wesley Reading, 1990.

Bowen, M. "Alcoholism as viewed through Family Systems Theory and Family Psychotherapy." *Annals of the New York Academy of Science* 223 (1974): 115-22.

Brown, S. *Treatment of Alcoholism—A Developmental Model of Recovery.* New York: Wiley and Sons, 1985.

Burk, E. D. "Some Contemporary Issues in Child Development and the Children of Alcoholic Parents." *Annals of the New York Academy of Science* 197 (1972): 189-95.

Burton, G., and H. M. Kaplan. "Marriage Counseling with Alcoholics and Their Spouses II: The Correlation of Excessive Drinking Behaviour with Family Pathology and Social Deterioration.". *Br. J. Addict* 63 (1968): 161-70.

Cermak, T. *A Primer on Adult Children of Alcoholics.* Pampano Beach: Health Care Communications, 1985.

Covington, S. *Women and Addiction - A Collection of Papers.* La Jolla, Calif. (self published) 1982.

Davis, Laura. *Allies in Healing.* New York: Harper Perennial, 1991.

E., Stephanie, "Shame-Faced Pamphlet". Center City, Minn.: Hazelden Foundation, 1986.

Edwards, Patricia, Cheryl Harvey, and Paul C. Whitehead. "Wives of Alcoholics: A Critical Review and Analysis." *Quarterly Journal of Studies on Alcohol* 34, no. 1 (1973): 112-32.

Hindman, M. "Family Therapy and Alcoholism." *Alcohol Health and Research World.* 1, no. 1 (Fall 1976): PAGES?.

Jackson, Joan K. "The Adjustment of the Family to the Crisis of Alcoholism." *Quarterly Journal of Studies on Alcohol* 15, no. 4 (1954): 562-86.

Jung, C. G. *The Collected Works of C. G. Jung.* Translated by Herbert Read, et al. Princeton: Billinger Series, 1954.

_______. *Memories Dreams and Reflections.* New York: Pantheon Books, 1961.

Kalff, Dora. *Sandplay.* Boston: Sigo Press. 1980.

Kirkpatrick, J. *Goodbye Hangover, Hello Life: Self-help for Women.* New York: Athenaeum, 1986.

Klagsbrun, M. and D. I. Davis. "Substance Abuse and Family Interaction." *Family Process* 16 (1977): 149-64.

Leonard, Linda. *Witness to the Fire. Creativity and the Veil of Addiction.* Boston Shambhala Publications, 1989.

McFarland, B. Sexuality and Recovery Center City, Minn.: Hazelden Foundation, 1984.

Mellody, Pia. *Facing Co-Dependence.* New York: Harper and Row, 1988.

Miller, Alice. *For Your Own Good:* Hidden Cruelty in Child Rearing and the Roots of Violence. New York: Farrer, Straus and Giroux, 1984.

Muir, Charles, Carolyn Muir, and Tantra. *The Art of Conscious Loving.* San Francisco: Mercury House, 1989.

O'Connell, K. *Children of Alcoholic Parents: Their Needs and Our Responsibility. Special Report to the National Institute on Alcoholism and Alcohol Abuse.* 1978.

_______. *End of the Line: Quitting Cocaine.* Philadelphia: Westminster Press, 1985.

_______. "Lust vs. Love." *Alcohol and the Addictions Magazin*e (January-February 1987).

_______. "Working Through it Together—Couples in Recovery." *Alcohol and the Addictions Magazine* (August 1986).

Orford, J., S. Guthrie, P. Nicholls, S. Oppenheimer, and C. Hensman. "Self-reported Coping Behaviour of Wives of Alcoholics and Its Association with Outcome." *Journal of Studies on Alcohol* 36 (1975): 1254-67.

Paolino, T. J., B. S. McCrady, and K. B. Kogan. "Alcoholic Marriages: A Longitudinal Empirical Assessment of Alternative Theories." *British Journal of Addiction* 73 (1978): 129-38.

Rees, Alwyn and Brinley Rees. *Celtic Heritage.* London: Thames and Hudson, 1961.

Scidda, Joan and Marsha Vannicelli, "Sex-Role Conflict and Women's Drinking." *Journal of Studies on Alcohol* 40, no. 1 (1979): 28-44.

Smith, C. G. "Marital Influence on the Treatment Outcome for Alcoholics." *Journal of the Irish Medical Association* (1967): 433-34.

Smolensky, William R, David W. Martin, Ronald J. Lorimar, and Ron N. Forthofer. "Leisure Behaviour and Attitudes toward Leisure of Alcoholics and Nonalcoholics." *Journal of Studies on Alcohol* 41, no. 3 (1980): 293-99.

Sjoo, Monica and Barbara Mor. *The Great Cosmic Mother.* San Francisco: Harper and Row, 1987.

Shame—Understanding and Coping. Center City, Minn.: Hazelden Foundation, 1981.

Warner, Rebecca H. and Henry L. Rosett. "The Effects of Drinking on Offspring: An Historical Survey of the American and British Literature." *Journal of Studies on Alcohol* 36, no. 11 (1975) 1395-1420.

Weinrib, Estella. *Image of the Self.* Boston: Sigo Press, 1983.

Weinbery, J. *Sex and Recovery.* Minneapolis: Recovery Press, 1977.

Whitmont, Edward and Sylvia Perera. *Dreams. A Portal to the Source.* New York: Routledge, 1989.

Wilsnack, S. C. "Sex Role Identity in Female Alcoholism". *Journal Abnormal Psychology* 82 (1973) 253-61.

Woititz, J. *Struggle for Intimacy.* Pompano Beach: Health Communications, 1985.

Wolin, Steven J., Linda A. Bennett, Denise L. Noonan, and Martha A. Teitelbaum. "Disrupted Family Rituals: A Factor in the Intergenerational Transmission of Alcoholism." *Journal of Studies on Alcohol* 41, no. 3 (1980): 199-214.

Woodman, M. The Ravaged Bridegroom. *Masculinity in Women.* Toronto: Inner City Books, 1990.

About the Author

While the facts are true in the anecdotes I present, the names of the people and other details have been changed to protect their privacy.

I enjoy hearing from people who are using the information in this book. I read each letter, although, I regret that I am unable to answer every letter personally.

I am available for consultations, workshops and speeches internationally regarding all aspects of healing discussed in this book. Feel free to contact me in care of the publisher to obtain my current telephone number and address for any inquiries:

Deaconess Press
2450 Riverside Ave. S.
Minneapolis MN 55454
Telephone: 1-800-544-8207